NATION BUILDING:
THE U.N. AND NAMIBIA

**NATIONAL DEMOCRATIC INSTITUTE
FOR INTERNATIONAL AFFAIRS**

NATIONAL DEMOCRATIC INSTITUTE FOR INTERNATIONAL AFFAIRS

The National Democratic Institute for International Affairs (NDI) conducts nonpartisan political development programs overseas. By working with political parties and other institutions, NDI seeks to promote, maintain and strengthen democratic institutions and pluralistic values in new and emerging democracies. NDI has conducted a series of democratic development programs in nearly 30 countries including Argentina, Bangladesh, Botswana, Brazil, Chile, Czechoslovakia, Haiti, Hungary, Namibia, Nicaragua, Northern Ireland, Panama, Pakistan, the Philippines, Poland, South Korea, Taiwan and Uruguay.

ISBN 1-880134-06-3: $6.95

TABLE OF CONTENTS

DISTRICTS

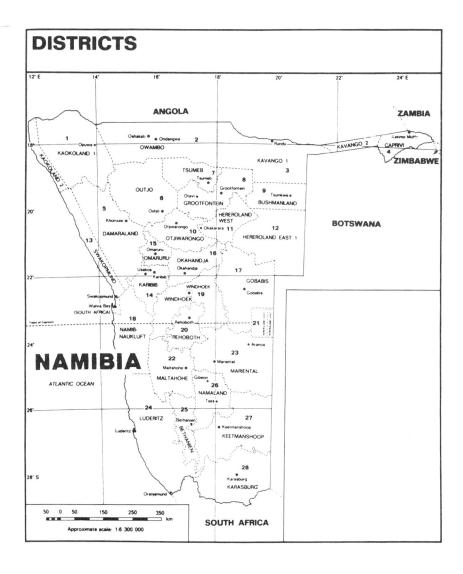

ANGOLA

ZAMBIA

1
KAOKOLAND 1
Opuwa ●

Oshakati ● ● Ondangwa 2
OWAMBO

Rundu ●

KAVANGO 2

CAPRIVI
4

ZIMBABWE

KAVANGO 1

3

TSUMEB 7
● Tsumeb

8
Grootfontein ●

OUTJO
6
Otavi ●
GROOTFONTEIN

9
Tsumkwe ●
BUSHMANLAND

5
Khorixas ●

Outjo ●

HEREROLAND
WEST

BOTSWANA

13
DAMARALAND

Otjiwarongo ●
10
OTJIWARONGO
15

● Okakarara 11

12
HEREROLAND EAST 1

Omaruru ●
OMARURU

OKAHANDJA
16

Usakos ●
KARIBIB
14

● Karibib

Okahandja ●
17

WINDHOEK
WINDHOEK
19

GOBABIS
Gobabis ●

Swakopmund ●
Wahis Bay
(SOUTH AFRICA)

18
NAMIB-
NAUKLUFT

Rehoboth ●
20
REHOBOTH

21

NAMIBIA

ATLANTIC OCEAN

22

● Aranos

23

Maltahohe ●
MALTAHOHE

● Mariental
MARIENTAL

Gibeon ●
26
NAMALAND
Tses ●

24
LUDERITZ

25

27

Luderitz ●

Bethanien ●
BETHANIEN

● Keetmanshoop
KEETMANSHOOP

28
Karasburg ●
KARASBURG

Oranjemund ●

50 0 50   150   250   350
km

Approximate scale: 1:6 300 000

SOUTH AFRICA

MAJOR ACTORS IN TRANSITION PROCESS

The United Nations, South Africa and the territory's two main political parties were the most important players in the Namibian transition. Other domestic and international organizations also played significant roles.

United Nations

Special Representative

Security Council Resolution 431 of 1978 authorized the UN Secretary-General to appoint a Special Representative (SR) for Namibia "in order to ensure the early independence of Namibia through free and fair elections under the supervision and control of the United Nations." (Appendix III.) Martti Ahtisaari of Finland has held the office since its creation in 1978. Prior to joining the UN, Ahtisaari served as Finland's ambassador to Tanzania, Zambia, Somalia and Mozambique. Ahtisaari also served as UN Commissioner for Namibia from 1977 to 1981. Effective January 1, 1987, UN Secretary-General Javier Perez de Cuellar appointed Ahtisaari as UN Under-Secretary-General for Administration and Management.

UNTAG

Security Council Resolution 435 of 1978 established the United Nations Transition Assistance Group (UNTAG), a joint civilian and military force, to assist the Special Representative in the implementation of the Resolution 435 Settlement Plan. As part of the civilian component, the Settlement Plan also established the UNTAG Civilian Police (CIVPOL) to monitor the activities of the South West Africa Police (SWAPOL).

Lieutenant General Dewan Prem Chand of India was designated the military force Commander in 1980. Ambassador Legwaila Joseph Legwaila of Botswana was appointed Deputy Special Representative in June 1989. Other senior UNTAG civilian officials included: Cedric Thornberry (Ireland), Director of the Office of the Special Representative; Hisham Omayad (Ghana), chief of the Electoral Division; Stephen Fanning (Ireland), Police Advisor and head of the civilian police; Abdou Ciss (Senegal), Director of Administration; John Rwambuya (Uganda), Director of the Oshakati region; and Kwame Opoku (Ghana), Senior Legal Advisor. The Special Representative also received advice about political prisoners from an independent jurist, Carl Norgaard (Denmark).

Secretary-General's Task Force

In April 1989, Secretary-General Perez de Cuellar formed a high-level task force in New York to advise him about events in Namibia. Four top UN officials composed the task force's core: Virendra Dayal (India), Chef de Cabinet; Marrack Goulding (U.K.), Under-Secretary-General for Special Political Affairs; Carl-August Fleischhauer (F.R.G.), Under-Secretary-General and Legal Counsel; and Abdulrahim Farah (Somalia), Under-Secretary-General, Department for Special Political Questions, Regional Cooperation, Decolonization and Trusteeship. In August, the task force sent Paul Szasz (U.S), a senior UN lawyer, to Namibia to assist the Special Representative in the negotiation of the final election law.

UNHCR

The UN High Commissioner for Refugees (UNHCR) was responsibile for the repatriation of Namibian refugees. Forty-two thousand Namibians who were exiled in more than 40 countries were resettled in the country between July and mid-September 1989. Nicholas Bwakira (Burundi) was in charge of the operation.

Republic of South Africa

Administrator-General

Appointed by the South African president, the Administrator-General (AG) maintained legislative and executive responsibilities for Namibia during the transition period, including administration of the election. President P.W. Botha appointed Louis Pienaar as the Administrator-General on July 1, 1985, and Pienaar continued to serve in that capacity during the transition period. Others in the administration who played a critical role were A.G. Visser, Chief of Registration and Elections; Kabus Bauermuster, Director of the AG's office; and Gerhard Roux, who was responsible for the government's voter education program and press relations.

Foreign Ministry

At various points during the transition, Foreign Minister R.F. (Pik) Botha and Ambassador to the United Nations Jeremy Shearer facilitated negotiations between the Special Representative and the Administrator-General. The ministry assigned Ambassador Karl von Hirschburg to Windhoek to handle some of the delicate and difficult negotiations, and to brief international observer groups.

Security Forces

Under the control of the AG, the South West Africa Police (SWAPOL) retained primary responsibility for maintaining law and order in the territory during the transition period. After the adoption of Resolution 435 in 1978, South African authorities created two new territorial security forces, the South West Africa Territorial Force (SWATF), which conscripted Namibians to operate in conjunction with the South African Defense Force (SADF), and the counterinsurgency police unit known as "Koevoet" (Afrikaans for crowbar), organized in 1979 by South African Colonel Hans Dreyer. Composed of South African officers and Ovambo recruits, Koevoet engaged in a ruthless counterinsurgency campaign in the north against SWAPO guerrillas and systematically intimidated SWAPO supporters before and during the transition period.

Namibian Political Parties

SWAPO

The South West Africa People's Organization (SWAPO) has been a prominent nationalist liberation movement for three decades. Founded in 1958 as the Ovamboland People's Congress, a Namibian nationalist workers movement, and reconstituted under its current name in 1960, SWAPO was recognized by the UN General Assembly in 1976 as the "sole and authentic" representative of the Namibian people. In accordance with Resolution 435, the UN on April 1, 1989, withdrew its recognition of SWAPO and terminated all financial support for SWAPO. The president of SWAPO, Sam Nujoma, returned to Namibia on September 14, 1989 for the first time in 30 years.

Democratic Turnhalle Alliance

The Democratic Turnhalle Alliance (DTA) is a multiracial coalition of parties founded in the wake of the South African-sponsored Turnhalle Conference in 1977. The DTA participated in the South African-sponsored Turnhalle government from 1979 to 1983 and in the Multi-Party Conference's "interim" government from 1985 to 1989. Dirk Mudge of the Namibian Republican Party was the DTA's principal founder and has served as chairman since its formation.

Namibian Organizations

Council of Churches
The Council of Churches in Namibia (CCN) comprises the seven major churches in Namibia, which represent about 80 percent of the population. The CCN is the only organization in the country with an effective nationwide communications network. During the transition, the CCN played a prominent role in the repatriation of refugees. As "an implementing partner" with the UN High Commissioner, the CCN was responsible for operating reception and support centers, providing transportation and distributing food and other goods. In addition, it established an independent election-monitoring unit, submitted formal comments on proposed electoral legislation, assisted with voter registration and transported people to the polls. Individual clergy members throughout the country facilitated the introduction and acceptance of UNTAG field personnel in the local communities. Although sympathetic to SWAPO, several church leaders affiliated with CCN were persistent in applying pressure for an accounting of alleged SWAPO political prisoners.

Namibian Peace Plan Study and Contact Group (NPP 435)
The NPP is a private nonpartisan local organization founded in 1986 by advocate Bryan O'Linn to promote and monitor the implementation of UN Resolution 435. In this capacity, the NPP has organized a series of multi-party seminars and symposia to stimulate debate among Namibia's various interest groups about the transition process. During the campaign, NPP also conducted an extensive and critical three-part study of Namibia's broadcast media.

International Community

Contact Group
The five Western members of the UN Security Council in 1978 -- Canada, France, the Federal Republic of Germany, the United Kingdom and the United States -- mediated negotiations and developed the settlement proposal that became the basis for UN Security Council Resolution 435. The Contact Group, particularly the United States, was also active in promoting subsequent agreements concerning the implementation of Resolution 435 and in monitoring the transition process.

Frontline States
Six African states on the "front line" with South Africa -- Angola, Botswana, Mozambique, Tanzania, Zambia and Zimbabwe -- coordinated

their diplomatic efforts with respect to the transition process. In addition, Nigeria often played a key supporting role. The Frontline states acted, in effect, as the political custodian for SWAPO. They were represented in Namibia by a permanent diplomatic mission of ambassadors from each of the respective governments.

Joint Commission

In December 1988, Angola, Cuba and South Africa established a Joint Commission to monitor compliance with the tripartite agreement among the three countries. The parties invited the United States and the Soviet Union to participate in the Commission as observers and agreed to invite Namibia to become a full member upon independence. Representatives of UNTAG and the AG's office also attended Joint Commission meetings as "invited guests." The Joint Commission played a key role after the events of April in moving the transition process back on track. Its Intelligence Subcommittee established "verification mechanisms" that played an important role in dealing with various allegations of impending invasions and destabilization from May to November 1989.

Organization of African Unity

The Organization of African Unity (OAU) is the regional intergovernmental organization of African states. Like the Frontline states, the OAU maintained a diplomatic mission in Namibia and took an active role in monitoring the process and in communicating with the Secretary-General and the Special Representative.

CHRONOLOGY OF EVENTS FOR NAMIBIA

1920   League of Nations grants Class C Mandate for South West Africa (SWA) to Union of South Africa.

1925   South Africa establishes constitution for SWA that grants administrative control to white population.

1946   UN requests South Africa conclude trusteeship agreement; South Africa seeks to incorporate SWA as fifth province.

1949   South Africa gives whites in SWA direct representation in South African Parliament.

1950   International Court of Justice (ICJ) rules that South Africa has no obligation to conclude a trusteeship agreement but holds that the mandate remain in effect.

1960   SWAPO formed under current name.

1964   Odendaal Commission recommends creation of "bantustans" in SWA.

1966   UN General Assembly revokes South Africa's mandate. SWAPO begins armed struggle.

1967   General Assembly creates UN Council for South West Africa and Commissioner for South West Africa to administer the territory.

1968   General Assembly adopts "Namibia" as the territory's name.

1969   Security Council Resolutions 264 and 269 recognize revocation of the mandate.

1971   ICJ upholds General Assembly's revocation of the mandate and declares that South Africa is obliged to withdraw from the territory.

1973   General Assembly grants observer status to SWAPO.

1976   Security Council adopts Resolution 385 calling for elections under UN supervision and control. General Assembly recognizes SWAPO as "sole and authentic" representative of the Namibian people. Turnhalle Conference of internal parties establishes interim government.

1977   Western Contact Group (United States, France, Canada, West Germany and the United Kingdom) begins efforts to mediate negotiations on an internationally acceptable settlement.

July   South Africa unexpectedly announces the end of SWA representation in the South Africa parliament and the appointment of an Administrator-General to administer affairs in Namibia.

November The General Assembly declares South Africa's annexation of Walvis Bay illegal, and a violation of the UN Charter and Declaration on Decolonization.

1978

February Proximity Talks held in New York with all relevant parties.

April   Contact Group submits settlement proposal to Security Council, under which South Africa would administer the elections under UN supervision and control.

July   Security Council Resolution 431 creates office of the Special Representative for Namibia and Resolution 432 mandates that Walvis Bay be reintegrated into Namibia. The Secretary-General immediately appoints Martti Ahtisaari Special Representative.

September Security Council passes Resolution 435 adopting the Settlement Plan and establishing UNTAG.

1980	Proclamation AG 8 creates ethnic administrative authorities in Namibia.
1981	U.S. announces policy linking implementation of Resolution 435 to withdrawal of Cuban troops from Angola.
1982	Proposal submitted to Secretary-General by Contact Group on principles to govern the electoral system and the constitution, and on actions to ensure UN and South African impartiality.
1983	Council of Ministers in Namibia resigns, and Administrator-General dissolves national assembly and resumes direct rule. Multi-Party Conference (MPC) convened in November.
1985	South African State President issues Proclamation R101, which cedes administrative responsibility to interim government formed by the MPC and adopts Bill of Rights.

1988

July	Agreement reached at Governor's Island on "principles for a peaceful settlement in south-western Africa" among Angola, Cuba and South Africa.
August	Protocol of Geneva establishes cease-fire and calls for implementation of Settlement Plan.
December	Protocol of Brazzaville on December 13 commits parties to treaties providing for implementation of Settlement Plan and phased withdrawal of Cuban troops from Angola and creating Joint Commission. Tripartite Accord signed in New York on December 22.

1989

January	Security Council Resolutions 628 and 629 set April 1 as implementation date for Resolution 435. Debate in Security Council over size of UNTAG force.

February	Security Council Resolution 632 approves Secretary-General's compromise over size of UNTAG force and authorizes implementation.
March	General Assembly approves UNTAG budget.
April	Implementation of Settlement Plan begins with outbreak of hostilities in northern Namibia. Joint Commission issues Mt. Etjo declaration on April 9, which calls for restoration of the cease-fire and provides for the withdrawal of SWAPO forces to Angola north of the 16th parallel. South African appointed Administrator-General proposes draft voter registration law.
May	Confinement to base of SADF and implementation process restored. Commission for the Prevention and Combating of Intimidation and Election Malpractices established on May 22.
June	Amnesty Proclamation, AG 13, and First Law Amendment (Abolition of Discriminatory or Restrictive Laws for purposes of Free and Fair Elections) Proclamation, AG 14, enacted on June 12. UNHCR begins repatriation of Namibians. Registration of Voters (Constituent Assembly) Proclamation, AG 19, enacted on June 28.
July	Voter registration begins on July 3. AG proposes draft election law on July 21.
August	Security Council Resolution 640 demands "strict compliance" with Resolutions 435 and 632 by all parties, "especially South Africa," and directs the Secretary-General to ensure that electoral legislation conforms to "internationally accepted norms."
September	Registration of Political Organizations, Proclamation, AG 43, enacted on September 4. Code of Conduct signed by nine political parties on September 12. Anton Lubowski assassinated on September 12. Sam Nujoma returns to

Namibia on September 14. Koevoet demobilized. Voter registration completed on September 23.

October   Election Proclamation, AG 49, enacted on October 13. UN Mission to investigate allegations about SWAPO detainees issues report on October 16.

November   Constituent Assembly Proclamation, AG 62, enacted on November 6. Elections begin on November 7 and balloting completed on November 11. AG announces election results on November 14 and SR certifies that the election process has been free and fair. Constituent Assembly meets for the first time on November 21.

1990

February   Constituent Assembly unanimously adopts constitution, designates March 21 as date for independence and elects Sam Nujoma as Namibia's first President.

March   Formal independence on March 21.

ACKNOWLEDGMENTS

The information in this study of the Namibian transition process was collected during the course of a year by representatives of the National Democratic Institute for International Affairs (NDI). The following individuals participated in one or more of NDI's five fact-finding missions to Namibia between March and November 1989 to observe various phases of the transition process: Merritt Becker, Joan Bingham, Eric Bjornlund, Alan Bowser, Byron Charlton, Frederic Cowan, Christopher Edley, Larry Garber, Alisdair Graham, Humayan Mohammed Kahn, Patricia Keefer, James King, Michael McAdams, Charles Mokobi, Katherine Moore, Amelia Parker, Donald Payne, Masipula Sithole, Dennis Smith and Maurice Tempelsman. NDI thanks them for their contributions to this study.

Eric Bjornlund, an attorney with previous experience in Namibia, is the principal author of this study. He was assisted at NDI by Patricia Keefer, Namibia Program Director; Larry Garber, Election Consultant; Mahnaz Ispahani, Research Director; and Katherine Moore, Program Assistant. Sue Grabowski, NDI Public Information Director, endured the multiple redrafting, editing and production.

This study would not have been possible without the assistance of a great many people who described their experiences and shared their insights. Many of these people are listed in Appendix I, but several deserve special thanks: Ambassador Donald McHenry, who provided the original initiative for NDI involvement in Namibia; United Nations Special Representative for Namibia Martti Ahtisaari, Director of the Special Representative's office Cedric Thornberry, and UNTAG Liaison Officer Peggy Kelley, who responded to NDI's many requests for information in a spirit of cooperation and support; and Marrack Goulding, UN Under-Secretary for Special Political Affairs, who arranged interviews with members of the Secretary-General's Namibian Task Force and others in the Secretariat in New York.

We also would like to acknowledge the advice, support and assistance we received from the Namibia Peace Plan Study and Contact Group (NPP 435), particularly Bryan O'Linn, the founder of the organization, Peter Koep, its Chairman, and Nahum Gorelick, its Executive Director.

J. Brian Atwood
NDI President

FOREWORD

Donald F. McHenry

The independence of Namibia marks the end of a long dispute between the United Nations and South Africa over the right of Namibians to exercise their right of self-determination. The process finally agreed upon was complex and was a test of the goodwill of all of the parties. In the end, Resolution 435, the formula under which Namibians voted in free and fair elections, proved to be more than adequate for the job. Namibians went to the polls in large numbers in an impressive display of their own determination to exercise the right to vote.

While the United Nations Transition Assistance Group under the guidance of Martti Ahtisaari, Special Representative of the UN Secretary-General, had the responsibility for ensuring that conditions leading to the election and the election itself were free and fair, it was both inevitable, appropriate, and helpful that outside groups in the form of observers should be involved in the elections. Some observer groups were objective, informed and helpful; others were clearly partisan and frequently unhelpful.

Few would disagree that the work of the National Democratic Institute for International Affairs (NDI) stood out among the most astutue and helpful observer groups, and appropriately so. NDI brought to the task seasoned students of democratic processes and a commitment to the establishment of, and improvement of, democratic institutions in Africa, as well as in Latin America and Europe.

Given the unique nature of the Namibia experience there no doubt will be many informed and scholarly studies in the years to come. What follows is NDI's highly useful and contemporary account of the final phase of the independence process in Namibia, together with insightful observations for improvements in future situations where, in the face of bitter dispute, the international community might play a role in helping install and build democratic institutions. As the authors correctly point out, the Namibia experience is a tribute to the United Nations at work. The successful outcome suggests that disputes about who governs need not flounder over an inability to agree upon who exercises authority while the people decide. For, once the parties are agreed upon the exercise of the vote, who governs during the decision process is less important that the terms and prevailing conditions of government and the ability of a respected outside authority to withhold its imprimatur at every step in the process.

PREFACE

Since its founding in 1983, the National Democratic Institute for International Affairs has worked on a nonpartisan basis in more than 25 countries, assisting the development of political parties, supporting free and fair elections, strengthening government institutions and promoting civic education. NDI places a priority on programs that can contribute to democratic development during periods of political transition.

NDI involvement in Namibia was encouraged by former U.S. Ambassador to the United Nations Donald McHenry and UN Special Representative for Namibia Martti Ahtisaari. An initial visit in March 1989 by NDI's President J. Brian Atwood and Senior Consultant Patricia Keefer, during which they conferred with prominent Namibians, set the stage for the Institute's multi-faceted program in support of the transition process. The year-long program included a critique of the proposed electoral system by election experts from several countries; various joint projects with Namibia Peace Plan 435 Study and Contact Group (NPP 435); fact-finding delegations that observed the registration and election processes; and an assessment of the UN role in the process.

The delegation of election experts visited Namibia between May 27 and June 4, while the registration law was under negotiation and as plans for the election system were being discussed. Senator Alisdair Graham of Canada led the delegation, which included public officials and political professionals from Barbados, Botswana, Pakistan, the United States and Zimbabwe. On June 4, after visiting seven regions of the territory, the delegation presented a preliminary report to the Special Representative. The report critiqued the proposed election system and recommended specific changes. As described in this report, after protracted negotiations between the Special Representative and the Administrator-General, many of the recommendations were adopted. NDI subsequently published a comprehensive delegation report, which was circulated to interested parties at the UN and to governments and nongovernmental organizations involved with the Namibia transition process.

NDI has worked actively with Namibia Peace Plan Study and Contact Group 435 (NPP 435), a local organization founded in 1986 to educate Namibians about the implementation of Resolution 435 and to work towards its early implementation. During the transition period, NPP 435 conducted a voter education program, monitored the coverage of the election campaign by the state-owned broadcasting company and organized a symposium to discuss the constitution for an independent Namibia. For the symposium, NDI sponsored U.S. Representative Donald Payne (D-NJ) as the keynote speaker.

NDI also observed the electoral process throughout the transition period. To this end, an NDI team visited different regions of Namibia in July during the registration period. Between October 31 and November 18, a seven-member team led by the Institute's president visited Namibia to observe the end of the election campaign, the balloting process in eight districts and the vote count in three district counting centers.

At the request of the chairmen of four U.S. Congressional subcommittees (Appendix II), NDI also assessed the role of the United Nations in the Namibian electoral process. The team present for the elections interviewed United Nations Transitional Assistance Group (UNTAG) officials; Namibian political party leaders; South African officials responsible for the transition; representatives of the churches, media, business community, trade unions, educational institutions and human rights organizations; diplomats based in Namibia; and others. These interviews were variously conducted in Windhoek, Namibia's capital; throughout the territory; and at UN headquarters in New York. NDI delegates also observed UNTAG supervisors in the field during the eight days of balloting.

This publication is a report of NDI's findings. It emphasizes the processes, both legal and operational. It is impossible in a work such as this to capture all of the political nuances. This analysis is based on NDI's first-hand experience and reports of those who were immediately involved. NDI intends to continue efforts to promote a pluralistic foundation for the world's newest nation.

Chapter 1
OVERVIEW

From November 7 to 11, 1989, the people of Namibia cast ballots in nationwide elections to determine their political future. Namibians elected delegates to a 72-member Constituent Assembly established to write a constitution for an independent Namibia. The Constituent Assembly has since adopted a final constitution and elected a president. On March 21, 1990, after 23 years of war and more than a century of colonization, Namibia finally achieved independence.

The December 1988 tripartite accord among Angola, Cuba and South Africa removed a longstanding impass created in part by the United States' desire to link the presence of Cuban troops in Angola to the negotiating process and in part by South Africa's intransigence. The accord made possible the elections which marked a milestone in Namibia's transition to independence. Thus, after more than a decade during which the fate of Namibian independence was delayed by a seemingly endless negotiating process, free and fair elections were conducted pursuant to the 1978 UN-sponsored Settlement Plan, UN Security Council Resolution 435.* The commitment, determination and tolerance of the Namibian people, and the acceptance of the results by

---

* Unless the context requires otherwise, this report uses the terms "Resolution 435" and "Settlement Plan" to refer collectively to the Contact Group's settlement proposal of April 10, 1978, the Secretary-General's report of August 29 and his explanatory statement of September 29, 1978, and the actual text of Security Council Resolution 435 of 1978. (Appendix IV.)

2

all parties, bode well for the emergence of democratic institutions in "Africa's last colony."

Free and Fair Elections

The success of the Namibian elections belied the gloomy predictions of those who doubted the possibility of a peaceful transition from colonial administration to democratic government. Notwithstanding widespread concerns about the potential for violence, fraud and delay, balloting and counting were peaceful, free and fair.

Most of the anticipated problems with the elections did not materialize. More than 97 percent of the registered voters cast ballots in the scheduled five days, despite the nearly universal expectation that five days would not be enough time. Similarly, the process of central verification and counting of "tendered" ballots did not delay tabulation of the results, which was completed in two days, one day less than expected. Likewise, a concern that Namibia's largely illiterate population would be unable to mark ballots properly never materialized; only a small number of ballots were rejected as spoiled. Finally, fears that violence would erupt during the balloting and tabulation processes went unrealized, although several violent incidents were reported after the announcement of the results.

Many people deserve credit for the success of these elections. The political parties worked together in the final weeks of the campaign to avoid violence, as they campaigned to give Namibians an opportunity to make a meaningful choice about the future of their country. The UN civilian, police and military forces helped to create an environment in which a reasonably free campaign could be conducted, despite the hostilities that developed during 23 years of armed conflict. The election administrators from the office of the Administrator-General and from UNTAG worked tirelessly and patiently in processing voters, sometimes under difficult conditions, through the five days of balloting. And, with the exception of problems with elements of the South African security apparatus, including the South West Africa Police (SWAPOL), the South African government and its Administrator-General ultimately proved willing to cooperate with the United Nations and the international community in the conduct of the elections.

In the final analysis, though, it was the people of Namibia, having waited so long for the opportunity to determine their own future, who made the process succeed. The responsible and patient conduct Namibians displayed throughout the election period was an inspiration for all who witnessed it. The international community can only hope that this lesson will resonate elsewhere in the world, including South Africa. The elections mark only a step in the development of democratic institutions in Namibia. The adoption of a constitution guaranteeing the rights of political parties, a free press, and an independent judiciary represents a second important step. The ultimate test of the Namibia transition experience will be the degree to which these democratic institutions are sustained over a period of time.

Election Results

In the elections, the South West Africa People's Organization (SWAPO) received 384,567 votes or about 57.3 percent of the 670,830 valid ballots cast. The Democratic Turnhalle Alliance (DTA) garnered some 191,532 votes or 28.6 percent. Under the election's proportional representation system, SWAPO earned 41 of the 72 seats in the Constituent Assembly and DTA captured 21. Other parties obtaining seats were the United Democratic Front of Namibia (37,874 votes; four seats), Action Christian National (23,728 votes; three seats), the National Patriotic Front (10,693 votes; one seat), the Federal Convention of Namibia (10,452 votes; one seat), and the Namibian National Front (5,344 votes; one seat). (Appendix V.)

On November 14, the UN Secretary-General's Special Representative for Namibia, Martti Ahtisaari, pursuant to his authority under Resolution 435, certified that the electoral process had been free and fair. (Appendix VI.) More important, all parties accepted the results of the elections, and within a week the Constituent Assembly commenced writing a constitution and forming a government. Despite the fact that SWAPO was denied the two-thirds mandate it had sought from the voters, the constitution was unanimously approved by the delegates to the Constituent Assembly.

United Nations

Under the leadership of the UN Special Representative for Namibia, the United Nations Transition Assistance Group (UNTAG) played a critical role in the Namibian electoral and transition process. UNTAG's very presence contributed substantially to a fundamental improvement in Namibia's political climate, a change that set the stage for the reality of free and fair elections. Through its efforts to facilitate national reconciliation, its participation in the development of an election system, its military and police monitoring operations, and its supervision of the registration, balloting and counting processes, UNTAG ensured that the elections obtained the confidence of -- and reflected the will of -- the Namibian people. The UNTAG operation was unprecedented. Its scale alone -- some 110 nationalities were represented in the UNTAG forces -- would have made it unusual. But UNTAG's de facto mandate -- nothing less than the promotion of political reconciliation in an effort to ensure a free and fair election -- represented a radical departure from past UN practice. UNTAG was loosely modeled on previous UN peacekeeping and election monitoring operations, but it sought to go beyond merely preserving the peace between hostile parties or passively observing an election. In addition to its innovation of police monitors, UNTAG, for the first time in UN history, combined an international military and civilian operation that actively sought to promote political change in order to create the reality of genuinely free and fair elections.

As described in this study, UNTAG confronted considerable challenges in implementing Security Council Resolution 435. Not the least of these was the fact that the Settlement Plan, which was a compromise to begin with, was more than a decade old and had been negotiated and drafted in the context of a set of local circumstances that had changed considerably. Nevertheless, none of the interested parties wanted to attempt a revision of the Plan for fear of reopening complex and divisive disputes and hopelessly bogging down efforts to initiate the transition. In the end, the Settlement Plan proved to be a resilient agreement that survived the challenges posed by inherent ambiguities, conflicting interpretations and changing circumstances.

Political pressure greatly hampered the implementation of the UN Settlement Plan. Fiscal concerns caused the permanent members of the Security Council to limit the scope of the operation. As a result, the countries of the non-aligned movement, particularly those in Africa, complained that limits placed on the operation coupled with efforts to ensure UN impartiality threatened to become an excuse for favoring South Africa in the implementation process.

Despite the difficulties it faced, the UN accomplished a great deal in Namibia. First, the elections occurred on time. This was no small feat given the delay in reaching agreement on the UNTAG budget; the disruptions caused by the events of April 1 (when South Africa responded with violence to the apparent infiltration of SWAPO guerrillas into northern Namibia); the difficulties involved in adopting the various laws governing the electoral process; and the lack of trust permeating Namibian political culture. Second, the electoral system achieved international acceptance. At each stage, as provided in Resolution 435, UNTAG officials refused to allow the electoral process to proceed until South African officials made the changes necessary to ensure that the elections would be, and would be perceived to be, free and fair.

Third, the last part of the campaign and the elections period took place in a relatively peaceful atmosphere. This was particularly impressive in light of a bitter legacy of armed conflict and oppression. By contrast, there were problems of intimidation and violence in the early months of the transition. UNTAG contributed to the greatly improved climate in several ways. The Special Representative (SR), supported by the Secretary-General, maintained pressure on South African authorities to address the problems of intimidation. He helped to defuse the potential for partisan violence by pressuring the Namibian political parties to adopt a code of conduct and by facilitating dialogue among the parties. The presence and persistence of the UNTAG civilian police also contributed to the substantial reduction in the level of violence and intimidation.

Fourth, UNTAG's presence gave Namibians confidence in the entire electoral process. UNTAG also provided important administrative assistance; UNTAG personnel helped administer the registration process, accompanying their South African counterparts to remote parts of the territory. UNTAG officials in Windhoek carefully reviewed the preparations for the elections. They demanded and obtained an internationally acceptable legal framework for the elections, and they monitored every step, from the designation of the polling sites to the printing of the ballots to the selection of polling officials. Through the daily briefings of its press spokesperson, UNTAG also provided credible and useful information to Namibians and the international community in an environment where rumor and exaggerations dominated the political discourse.

Finally, the more than 1,700 election supervisors drawn from UN member states were active participants in the process during the seven days of balloting and counting. In addition to inspiring confidence and preventing fraud, they helped to complete the balloting and counting more quickly than had been anticipated.

Resolution 435 injected substance into the principle of free elections established by the Universal Declaration of Human Rights. In effect, the

UN developed and applied standards that went beyond the limited formula of the Universal Declaration, to ensure that the Namibian elections occurred in a free environment with administratively fair rules. The success of the UN-supervised elections in Namibia also signifies the growing importance of an internationally recognized legal framework for free and fair elections.

While UNTAG's accomplishments were extensive, significant problems did arise during the transition. Several were specific to Namibia; others reflect the UN's institutional problems.

First, the military conflict at the beginning of April 1989, which caught UNTAG unprepared, cast a cloud on the Resolution 435 process. Even after the transition process was rescued, the events of April continued to have repercussions that substantially disrupted and delayed the timetable for the implementation of the Settlement Plan and, in some quarters, eroded confidence in UNTAG and the Special Representative.

Second, UNTAG failed to obtain the complete cooperation of SWAPOL in investigating incidents of intimidation; these incidents continued to be a serious problem up until the last few weeks of the campaign. Notwithstanding the substantial difficulties, UNTAG might have been more aggressive, particularly in the first few months of the transition, in demanding the cooperation of SWAPOL.

Third, while the Special Representative understandably sought to establish a cooperative working relationship with the Administrator-General (AG) and to keep the transition process moving forward, he drew criticism for his seemingly tentative initial response to the AG's draft laws governing the electoral process; these laws would have created a system unacceptable to the international community. In response to widespread criticism, the Special Representative eventually insisted on substantial modifications. Although the laws ultimately incorporated virtually all of the changes the SR sought, the delay in the promulgation of the definitive election law until October 13, only 25 days before the first day of balloting, threatened the credibility of the process.

The Special Representative faced an extraordinarily complex task. On the one hand, he was obliged to guarantee that the elections take place in an environment that was fully free, under a system that was completely fair, and -- significantly -- to the satisfaction of the international community as well as the Namibian people. On the other hand, he was under great pressure to ensure that the process advanced according to an agreed upon timetable. The perceived importance of holding the elections on time spurred the SR to maintain momentum. While some observers criticized Ahtisaari for an alleged reluctance to exercise his authority, others defended his approach as one of timely engagement in strict accordance with the Resolution 435 mandate. The UN Secretary-General's task force, established in response to the developments of April 1, subjected the Special Representative to significant oversight from New York, which circumscribed his freedom to operate. The task force maintained daily contact with Ahtisaari and attempted to review his every decision. They believed that such close contact was necessary in order to keep the Secretary-General informed about developments in Namibia and to share with the Special Representative the continuing concerns of the international community. Coincidentally, while the task force may have presented something of an operational problem for Ahtisaari, it also increased his leverage; in negotiations with the Administrator-General, Ahtisaari could always blame New York for the harder line.

In the end, UNTAG's success represented a personal triumph for Martti Ahtisaari. Ahtisaari's diplomatic style of management promoted confidence in the process. His resolute manner in the face of tremendous and conflicting political pressures ultimately led to free and fair elections for Namibia and strengthened the credibility of the UN. In this regard, the Special Representative was a microcosm of UNTAG as a whole; the dedication and professionalism of all of the UNTAG personnel contributed to the United Nations' success in Namibia.

Role of Other Observers

Representatives of various governments and intergovernmental and nongovernmental organizations contributed to the implementation of Resolution 435 by monitoring the different phases of the transition process. Many observers arrived long before the campaign began, with several organizations establishing permanent presences soon after the transition commenced. As a result, they were able to receive and evaluate complaints, study proposed laws and raise matters with the Special Representative. In this sense, they assumed some of the responsibilities normally exercised by indigenous political parties.

Because of the activities of these observer groups, complaints of intimidation were communicated worldwide and the problems with proposed legislation were vigorously debated. However, in their advocacy, many observers aligned themselves with one or the other political party, thus jeopardizing their legitimacy as objective critics.

Future UN Operations

The turbulent international political environment of the 1990s and the success of UNTAG in Namibia have increased interest in the organization's potential role in the supervision and administration of elections. Lessons from UNTAG's operations in Namibia are valuable in the context of other regions where armed conflict or political polarization have frustrated efforts to resolve conflicts and to promote democratic governance. UNTAG could provide an adaptable model for areas where internationally-supervised elections have been suggested as a means of resolving seemingly intractable conflicts: Afghanistan, Cambodia, the Middle East, Sudan and the Western Sahara. While the situation in Namibia was unique, the UN's framework and implementation strategy for achieving independence in Namibia could, with appropriate adjustments, be transferable to other situations.

At the same time the UN was conducting its Namibia operation, it was also observing the electoral process in Nicaragua, in anticipation of the country's February 25, 1990 election. This occasion marked the first time the UN observed elections in a sovereign country, as opposed to a non-self-governing territory. While the effort in Nicaragua was substantially more limited than the Namibia operation, and the UN's mandate was significantly narrower, the Nicaragua mission provides further evidence of the UN's ability to play a constructive role in supporting free and fair elections.

The success of the UN's transition assistance operation in Namibia and its election observation effort in Nicaragua represent a significant step forward in demonstrating the UN's institutional capacity to resolve disputes and to make a major contribution to world peace.

Chapter 2
BACKGROUND

Namibia, formerly known as South West Africa, is a vast territory in the southwestern part of the African continent on the Atlantic coast. It is bounded by South Africa on the south, Botswana on the east, and Angola and Zambia on the north. Two large deserts compose much of the territory's land area: the Namib, which runs along the coast; and the Kalahari, which is further inland and extends into Botswana.

The territory's natural resources include mineral deposits of diamonds, copper, uranium, zinc and manganese, and vast fish resources off the coast. The more populated north receives more rainfall than other parts of the country, but is still very arid and barely supports a subsistence pastoral economy.

The modern sector of Namibia's economy is based on mining and cattle and karakul sheep ranching. There is little manufacturing. The economy is highly dependent on South Africa; South African multinational corporations control the commercial exploitation of Namibia's resources; the South African rand is the unit of currency; the territory is a member of the South African Customs Union; and the trade and communications infrastructure is oriented toward the Republic. South Africa also retains control of Walvis Bay, the only deepwater port along the Namibian coast.

With a population estimated at between 1.3 and 1.5 million and a land area of 319,000 square miles, Namibia is one of the world's most sparsely populated territories. It is roughly equal in area to France and Germany combined. More than half of the population lives in the 30,000 square miles of Ovamboland, located in northern Namibia bordering Angola. About 115,000 people live in the capital city of Windhoek, including the majority of the white population.

Ethnic groups that constitute the native African population of Namibia include the Ovambo, Kavango, Herero, Damara, Nama, Caprivi, Rehoboth Baster, Bushmen and Tswana. The Ovambos are the largest group, close to half of the total population. Whites comprise about seven percent of the population. About half of the 80,000 whites are Afrikaners; the rest are of English, German and Portuguese descent.

Under South African administration, Namibia recognized two official languages, Afrikaans and English, but English became the sole official language upon independence. Other major languages are Kwanyama, Ndonga, Herero, Nama, German and Bushman. An estimated 60 percent of the population is illiterate.

The earliest inhabitants of the territory were the nomadic San hunters and gatherers, now referred to as Bushmen. Damara and Nama peoples also settled in the area during the pre-colonial period.

European traders and missionaries arrived in Namibia in the mid-19th century. European intervention exacerbated inter-ethnic conflict, and in 1880, ostensibly to protect German subjects in the area, German Chancellor Otto von Bismarck took steps to establish German authority. Two years earlier, the British annexed Walvis Bay, an enclave inside the territory on the coast, and transferred the claim to the Cape Colony six years later.

In 1884, Germany declared a protectorate over the area surrounding Luderitz Bay along the southern coast. Two years later, the Germans negotiated with Portugal the boundary between German South West Africa (SWA) and Angola. In 1890, Germany and Britain set the boundary between SWA and the Bechuanaland Protectorate (now Botswana); the British also ceded a narrow ribbon of land, the Caprivi Strip, to give German South West Africa access to the Zambezi River.

German colonialism was particularly oppressive to the indigenous tribes and provoked periodic Herero and Nama revolts. The Herero, under Chief Maharero, initially agreed to a treaty of protection with Germany, but the leading Nama Chief, Hendrik Witbooi, refused such an agreement and attacked German encampments and supply convoys during the early 1890s. Germany finally forced Witbooi to surrender in 1894.

In 1904, German confiscation of land and cattle spurred the Herero to rebel. During the ensuing conflict, the German military commander, General Lothar von Trotha, issued an order for the extermination of the Hereros. Meanwhile, the Namas again took up arms. By 1907, however, the Germans crushed the rebellions and herded many of the surviving

Herero and Nama people into concentration camps. The extermination order against the Herero very nearly succeeded; almost 80 percent of the Herero population died as a result of military actions or privation. Because the Ovambos refused to aid the Hereros in the war with the Germans, hostile relations between the two ethnic groups continue today.

During World War I, South Africa invaded German South West Africa. The last of Germany's troops surrendered in 1915.

History of International Involvement

The post-war Peace Conference rejected South Africa's request to annex South West Africa. In 1920, however, the League of Nations entrusted South Africa with a Class C Mandate over the territory. The mandate obligated South Africa to administer the territory to "promote to the utmost the material and moral well-being, and the social progress of the inhabitants," and the League of Nations Covenant stated that the "well-being and development of such peoples form a sacred trust of civilization." In 1925, South Africa promulgated a constitution for the territory that mandated administrative control to the white population. The new constitution established a legislative assembly and an Administrator-General, with the latter exercising executive authority.

After World War II, the United Nations assumed supervisory authority over South West Africa. The UN General Assembly rejected South Africa's renewed plea to incorporate South West Africa as a fifth province, and South Africa refused to place the territory under the new international trusteeship system. Upon its ascension to power in 1948, the South African National Party gave whites in the territory direct representation in the Republic of South Africa's parliament and threatened to incorporate South West Africa unilaterally.

In 1950, the International Court of Justice ruled that South Africa had no obligation to conclude a trusteeship agreement with the UN, but held also that the mandate was still in force and that South Africa had no right to unilaterally change the territory's international status. Ten years later, Ethiopia and Liberia, the only sub-Saharan African members of the League of Nations, challenged South African control of Namibia in the International Court of Justice. In July 1966, a divided court ruled that Ethiopia and Liberia lacked standing to make the challenge. Acting in the wake of the World Court decision, the United Nations General Assembly revoked South Africa's mandate and declared the territory to be the direct responsibility of the UN.

Having thus formally passed legal responsibility for the territory to the international community, the General Assembly created the UN Council for South West Africa and established the office of the UN Commissioner for the territory in 1967. The Assembly adopted "Namibia" as the territory's name the following year. The Security Council, by Resolutions 264 and 269, endorsed the General Assembly's actions in 1969. Two years later, the International Court of Justice upheld the General Assembly's revocation of the mandate and declared that South Africa was obligated to withdraw its administration and end its occupation of the territory. South Africa, however, ignored the Court's and UN's actions and continued administering the territory as before.

Internal Developments

SWAPO, the leading Namibian national liberation organization, was founded in 1958 as the Ovamboland People's Congress and was renamed in 1960. In 1966, SWAPO adopted a policy of "armed struggle" against South African occupation following the decision of the International Court. The General Assembly granted SWAPO observer status as an "authentic" representative of the Namibian people in 1973 and recognized SWAPO as the "sole and authentic" representative of the Namibian people in 1976.

During the 1960s, South Africa took steps pursuant to the so-called Odendaal Plan to impose "separate development" in South West Africa. In 1968, the government established homelands for the native African population and authorized each homeland to establish legislative and executive councils.

In 1975, responding to internal and international pressure, Pretoria convened a constitutional conference of Namibian tribal leaders at the Turnhalle building in Windhoek. SWAPO and other small parties did not participate, opposing all efforts to move toward independence without the consent of the international community and the UN. After months of discussion, the so-called Turnhalle Conference reached agreement on an interim government and set December 31, 1976 as the target date for independence. The date for independence set at Turnhalle was not met, and for much of the next 15 years South Africa continued unilateral efforts to reach an internal settlement.

Chapter 3

RESOLUTION 435: FROM ADOPTION TO IMPLEMENTATION

The UN Security Council in 1976 adopted Resolution 385, which called for "free elections under the supervision and control of the United Nations." (Appendix VII.) South Africa objected to the plan, however, and proceeded with elections under the Turnhalle process. Thereafter, five Western members of the Security Council -- Canada, France, Federal Republic of Germany, the United Kingdom and the United States (the Contact Group) -- began mediating negotiations to reach an internationally acceptable solution.

In July 1977, South Africa unexpectedly announced the end of South West Africa representation in the South African parliament and the appointment of an Administrator-General to administer affairs in Namibia. The Contact Group had requested this step as one of several necessary to prepare for the transition to independence, but agreement had not been reached on many other issues. Negotiations continued during the remainder of 1977, which led to a meeting of all parties for "proximity talks" in New York in February 1978.

On April 10, 1978, the Contact Group submitted to the Security Council a compromise settlement proposal. The proposal represented an interpretation of Resolution 385 under which South Africa would administer Namibian elections subject to UN supervision and control. In the elections, Namibians would choose delegates to a Constituent Assembly that would prepare and adopt a constitution for an independent and sovereign Namibia.

In July, Security Council Resolution 431 requested the Secretary-General appoint a Special Representative for Namibia and submit a report making recommendations about the implementation of a settlement proposal in accordance with Resolution 385. The Secretary-General immediately appointed Martti Ahtisaari, the UN Commissioner for Namibia at the time, as his Special Representative (SR).

After the newly appointed Special Representative undertook a survey mission to Namibia in August, the Secretary-General recommended the acceptance of the Contact Group's plan and the establishment of a combined military and civilian force -- the United Nations Transition Assistance Group (UNTAG) -- to assist the Special Representative in the implementation of the plan. Based on the SR's consultations with Namibian political parties, the Secretary-General also concluded that there was not enough time to achieve independence by the December 31, 1978 target date; the plan required approximately seven months to complete the preparatory stages in an orderly fashion and a free and fair electoral campaign would take additional months. On September 29, 1978, after the Secretary-General submitted a further explanatory statement based on discussions with the interested parties, the Security Council adopted the settlement proposal as the UN plan for the independence of Namibia.

For more than a decade, Resolution 435 framed the debate about Namibian independence and formed the legal basis for the transition process. The resolution incorporated the details of the Contact Group proposal and the Secretary-General's reports by reference; the text expressly "approve[d]" the Secretary-General's August 29 report regarding the implementation of the settlement proposal and his September 29 explanatory statement. It established UNTAG for a maximum period of 12 months and repeated the Special Representative's earlier mandate "to ensure the early independence of Namibia through free elections under the supervision and control of the United Nations."

Unlike Resolution 385, which did not define the phrase, the Settlement Plan defined "supervision and control" to mean that the "Special Representative will have to satisfy himself at each stage as to the fairness and appropriateness of all measures affecting the political process at all levels of administration before such measures take effect." This implicitly recognized that South Africa, rather than the UN, would administer the elections, but it also established the UN's veto power as a control mechanism.

With regard to the elections, the Settlement Plan required that every adult Namibian be eligible "without discrimination or fear of intimidation" to vote, campaign and stand for election. It required a secret ballot with provisions for those unable to read and write. It mandated prompt development of an election system that would give all parties a "full and fair opportunity to organize and participate in the electoral process" with guarantees of freedom of speech, assembly, movement and press. The plan further ordered the repeal of all remaining discriminatory laws and the release of all political prisoners. It required that Namibian refugees be permitted to return to the territory.

Regarding the military situation, the Settlement Plan required a "comprehensive cessation of all hostile acts" and "the restriction of South African and SWAPO armed forces to base." It called for a phased withdrawal of South African troops within 12 weeks of implementation, but permitted 1,500 troops to remain restricted to base in the territory until the certification of the election results. It also called for the demobilization of citizen and ethnic forces. The plan left primary responsibility for law and order with existing police forces (i.e., those under South African control).

The Settlement Plan did not address the status of Walvis Bay, which South Africa claimed. The proposal deferred negotiations over Walvis Bay until after independence, but the Security Council stated unequivocally in Resolution 432 that Walvis Bay was an "integral part" of Namibia and must be reintegrated into the territory in order to assure Namibia's "territorial integrity and unity."

For many supporters of Namibian independence, Resolution 435 represented a sell-out. It implicitly recognized South African authority over the territory, notwithstanding the reiteration in the resolution that the UN objective "is the withdrawal of South Africa's illegal administration from Namibia." These critics also argued that providing South Africa with a role in administering the process guaranteed that the elections would be delayed and would not be conducted in a manner permitting the will of the people to be expressed.

On the other side, there were those who objected to the extensive UN role. These critics argued that, given UN membership, the organization was hardly in a position to guarantee or evaluate the fairness of the elections. Further, the UN was viewed as partisan, having endorsed SWAPO as the "sole and authentic" representative of the Namibian people.

Internal Elections

After first agreeing to Resolution 435, the South African government on September 20, 1978 decided to proceed unilaterally with plans for Constituent Assembly elections pursuant to the Turnhalle process without any international involvement. Elections were held in December 1978, but the Security Council declared them null and void. The Democratic Turnhalle Alliance (DTA), a coalition of 10 political parties formed by the Turnhalle Conference, won 41 of the 50 seats with 82 percent of the vote.

In May 1979, South Africa granted legislative authority to the assembly, but denied it power to declare independence. The following year executive authority was vested in a council of ministers, and the Namibia national assembly adopted Proclamation AG 8, a new constitution that separated the country into different ethnic groups for purposes of "second-tier" administration. Local elections were held for the 10 ethnically-based regional governments created by AG 8.

In 1983, after various disputes arose between the Administrator-General (AG) and the council of ministers the DTA led a revolt, whereby the entire council resigned ostensibly over the AG's veto of a bill on national holidays. The AG then dissolved the national assembly and the council, and resumed direct rule.

The Regional Military Conflict and the Doctrine of Linkage

In 1966, SWAPO launched an "armed struggle" against South African occupation. Over the next two decades, operating from bases in southern Angola and Zambia, SWAPO's military wing, the People's Liberation Army of Namibia (PLAN), engaged in sporadic guerrilla fighting with South African forces. After Angola gained independence from Portugal in 1975, war broke out between the Angolan government and the insurgent National Union for the Total Independence of Angola (UNITA).

During the late 1970s, Cuba sent troops to help the Angolan government and the South Africa Defense Force (SADF) began to support UNITA. Because SWAPO operated near regions of southern Angola controlled by UNITA and because of the SADF's support of UNITA, the Angolan war and the Namibian conflict became substantially intertwined. The Angolan war continued throughout the 1980s and UNITA forces continued to control sizeable areas of the southern part of that country.

After the adoption of Resolution 435, South Africa raised a number of objections to the plan, particularly the alleged bias of the United

Nations toward SWAPO. [There followed negotiations over a demilitarized zone along the Angolan-Namibian border.] Meanwhile, in 1981, the Reagan Administration adopted a policy of "linkage," pursuant to which the withdrawal of Cuban troops from Angola became a precondition for implementation of the Settlement Plan. By 1982, South Africa had made linkage a cornerstone of its resistance to the implementation of Resolution 435.

Critics assailed the concept of "linkage" and the efforts of the Contact Group -- especially the United States -- to negotiate further compromises with South Africa. In 1983, because of linkage, France disassociated from the Contact Group; it was soon followed by Canada and Germany. At summit meetings in Lusaka in September 1982 and in Harare in February 1983, the Frontline states and SWAPO issued communiques that demanded the decolonization process in Namibia be separated from the issue of Cuban troops in Angola. At New Delhi in March 1983, the non-aligned movement also "categorically rejected" linkage. SWAPO and its allies argued that, under international law, the right of Namibians to self-determination could not be held hostage to the military actions and political decisions of other countries. Further, it was South African military aid to UNITA that brought Cuban troops to Angola in the first place. The Secretary-General also emphasized, as stated in a November 1985 letter to the South African foreign minister, that "the Security Council itself has, on more than one occasion, rejected the linking of the independence of Namibia to irrelevant and extraneous issues."

Subsequent Agreements

Continuing negotiations resulted in several supplementary agreements. Most important was the agreement on constitutional and electoral principles and the secret agreement on impartiality, both reached in 1982. In 1985, the parties made an additional agreement regarding proportional representation.

1982 Constitutional Principles

In 1982, the Contact Group and the parties to the Namibian conflict agreed to supplement Resolution 435 with a mandatory set of principles to govern the Constituent Assembly's preparation of a constitution. (Appendix VIII.) As the Secretary-General stressed in January 1989, this agreement was part of the Resolution 435 process and binding on the parties. The agreement adopted principles applicable to the Constituent Assembly elections and to the constitution.

For the Constituent Assembly elections mandated by Resolution 435, the 1982 agreement restated the principles of the Settlement Plan: 1) universal adult suffrage; 2) a secret ballot with provisions for the illiterate; 3) an electoral system that would give all parties an opportunity to organize and participate; 4) freedom of speech, assembly, movement and press; and 5) an electoral system that would ensure fair representation of each party gaining substantial support in the election. The principles also required the Constituent Assembly to adopt the new constitution by a two-thirds majority.

With respect to the constitution itself, the principles required: 1) a "unitary, sovereign and democratic state"; 2) the recognition of the constitution as "the supreme law of the state" subject to amendment only by designated procedures; 3) a system of government with three bodies -- elected executive and legislative branches and an independent judiciary; 4) an electoral system consistent with the principles governing the Constituent Assembly elections; 5) a bill of rights, enforceable by judicial review, which would include specified rights; 6) the prohibition of criminal offenses with retroactive effect; 7) the "balanced structuring" of, and equal access to, the civil service and the police and defense forces; and 8) provision for elected local and/or regional administrations.

Impartiality Provisions

In September 1982, the Frontline states, Nigeria, SWAPO and the Contact Group reached agreement on steps to ensure the UN's impartiality in the process. The agreement was not made public at the time, however, and the only documentary evidence of the agreement was an "informal checklist" (Appendix IX) that the parties presented to the Secretary-General. The Secretary-General publicly acknowledged the existence of the agreement in reports issued in August 1983 and January 1989, and in May 1989 made the checklist public by officially submitting it to the General Assembly.

The impartiality agreement provided, *inter alia*, that only the Administrator-General and the Special Representative "will exercise authority during the transition period" -- because existing internal governmental structures were null and void under Resolution 435 -- and "will do so impartially." It stated that the future Security Council enabling resolution "should emphasize [the] responsibility of all concerned to cooperate to ensure impartial implementation of the Settlement Plan." It directed the Secretary-General to review all UN programs and to seek cooperation of specialized agencies to ensure impartial administration. It specified that none of the parties to the election or the ceasefire would be permitted to speak at the Security Council meeting authorizing the implementation of Resolution 435 and that the General Assembly would suspend consideration of Namibia during the transition period. Furthermore, the UN would not provide funds for SWAPO or any other party during the transition period, the UN Council for Namibia would stop all public operations, and the Commissioner for Namibia would suspend political activities. SWAPO would voluntarily forego the exercise of special privileges granted by the General Assembly, including participation as an official observer.

Multi-Party Conference and Interim Government

In November 1983, South Africa convened the Multi-Party Conference (MPC), another constitutional convention of internal political parties and ethnic organizations. As with the Turnhalle Conference, SWAPO did not participate. The MPC proposed the establishment of an "interim" government, the "Transitional Government of National Unity."

On June 17, 1985, South African President P.W. Botha issued Proclamation R101, pursuant to which the Administrator-General ceded administrative responsibility for internal affairs to the transitional government proposed by the MPC. In the transitional government, the AG acted on the advice of a cabinet, with legislative authority again vested in a national assembly. However, both the AG and the South African State President retained a veto over legislation. South Africa also retained direct control of foreign affairs and defense matters.

The MPC gave the DTA 22 of the 62 seats in the new national assembly and granted eight seats each to the SWAPO-Democrats (a small political party opposed to SWAPO), the Labor Party, the National Party of SWA, the Rehoboth Free Democratic Party and the South West African National Union. The interim government appointed a constitutional council to draft a new constitution, but the council never reached agreement and neither the MPC government nor Pretoria proceeded with internal plans for independence. The interim government continued until it was dissolved prior to implementation of the Settlement Plan in 1989.

Tripartite Accords

During 1987 and 1988, the combatants in the Angolan and Namibian conflicts fought to a military stalemate in southern Angola. UNITA and SADF forces stalled a major summer offensive of the Angolon government and Cuban forces, but the Angolans and Cubans in turn withstood a protracted siege in a bloody battle for Cuito Cuanavale in southern Angola and inflicted significant casualties on South African troops in a May 1988 battle. The Cubans also appeared poised to cut off SADF forces from the Namibian border and attacked a major dam on the Angolan side of border, which threatened northern Namibia's water supply.

With the military situation deadlocked, negotiations for a regional settlement in southwestern Africa gained momentum during 1988. In an attempt to achieve a breakthrough toward regional peace the U.S. government arranged, with support from the Soviet Union, for delegations from Angola, Cuba and South Africa to meet in London, Cairo and New York between May and August.

On July 13 at Governor's Island in New York, the parties reached an agreed statement of principles for a regional settlement. (Appendix X.) These principles established a ceasefire and called, *inter alia*, for the implementation of Resolution 435; the redeployment toward the north and the staged withdrawal of Cuban troops from Angola; respect for the sovereignty and territorial integrity of states; abstention from the use or threat of force; and verification and monitoring of compliance. On August 5 in Geneva, all sides agreed to a protocol establishing an immediate ceasefire and creating a joint military monitoring commission, comprised of representatives of all three countries, to monitor the Angolan-Namibian border. (Appendix XI.) They also recommended to the UN Secretary-General that the implementation of Resolution 435 commence on November 1, 1988. In a letter to the UN Secretary-General, President Sam Nujoma indicated that SWAPO, although not a signatory to the agreement, would observe the Geneva ceasefire agreement. (Appendix XII.)

Over the course of the fall, the parties met a number of times in Brazzaville, Congo to negotiate the final details of treaties to implement the settlement. There were extensive discussions, in particular, on the timetable for Cuban withdrawal. Finally, on December 13, the parties reached agreement and signed the Protocol of Brazzaville, which committed them to two treaties: a trilateral pact among Angola, Cuba and South Africa providing for the implementation of Resolution 435 beginning on April 1, 1989 and a related bilateral treaty between Angola and Cuba providing for the phased withdrawal of Cuban troops to be completed by mid-1991. (Appendix XIII.)

In an annex to the protocol, the parties formally established the Joint Commission "as a forum for discussion and resolution of issues regarding the interpretation and implementation of the tripartite agreement." The parties invited the United States and the Soviet Union to participate in the Commission as observers and agreed to invite Namibia to become a full member upon independence.

The protocol also provided that, prior to signing the treaties, Angola and Cuba would have to reach agreement with the Secretary-General on verification arrangements. Accordingly, on December 20, the Security Council established the United Nations Angola Verification Mission (UNAVEM) to verify the redeployment and phased withdrawal of Cuban troops in accordance with the agreement.

Representatives of the Angolan, Cuban and South African governments formally signed the treaties in New York on December 22, 1988. (Appendix XIV.) Under the tripartite agreement, the parties agreed to "immediately request the Secretary-General to seek authority from the Security Council to commence implementation" of Resolution 435.

Security Council Debate on UNTAG

The Security Council, by Resolutions 628 and 629 on January 16, 1989, officially welcomed the signing of the agreements among Angola, Cuba and South Africa and set April 1 as the implementation date for Resolution 435. The parties arrived at the April 1 date at least in part because the Settlement Plan contemplated a seven-month period between the beginning of implementation and the elections, and because elections could not be held after November without facing serious logistical problems posed by the rainy season.

Even as the UN endorsed the April 1 date, however, serious concern emerged in the Security Council about the cost and appropriate size of the UNTAG military contingent; consequently, Resolution 629, adopted at the behest of the permanent members, requested the Secretary-General identify cost-saving measures. Although it was never certain in 1978 that the total number of 7,500 troops would be necessary, in the context of the circumstances of 1989 the non-aligned movement, the

Organization of African Unity (OAU), the Frontline states and SWAPO strongly urged that the full military force be deployed.

The Secretary-General formally proposed a compromise. Although the authorized upper limit for the military force was to remain at the 7,500 number provided by Resolution 435, the initial size of the force would be set at 4,650. At the same time, the Secretary-General reserved the right to return to the Security Council for approval of additional troops if they proved necessary. This formula reduced the estimated cost of the operation from about $700 million to $416 million.

In a January 1989 report, the Secretary-General detailed how UNTAG would implement the Settlement Plan and increased the number of UNTAG civilian police from the 360 originally called for in the 1978 plan to 500. On February 16, 1989, the Security Council adopted Resolution 632, which approved the Secretary-General's January report and simultaneously authorized the implementation of Resolution 435 "in its original and definitive form to ensure conditions in Namibia which will allow the Namibian people to participate freely and without intimidation in the electoral process under the supervision and control of the United Nations."

On March 1, the General Assembly approved the UNTAG budget. On March 10, 20 days before the transition was to begin, the United Nations and South Africa executed an agreement concerning the juridical status of UNTAG. In this agreement, South Africa agreed that UNTAG personnel in Namibia would have legal immunity, and the UN agreed that UNTAG members would refrain from political or other activity incompatible with UN impartiality. The agreement also covered UNTAG facilities, vehicles and equipment; entry, residence and departure of UNTAG personnel; identification, uniform and arms; and similar matters.

After more than a decade, implementation of the Settlement Plan was finally at hand. But the debate over the size and cost of the UNTAG force substantially reduced the time available for UNTAG to plan for implementation. The dilatory pace of consultations and debate on the issue significantly hindered UNTAG's development of operational capability.

Events of Early April

The Namibian transition began in an inauspicious manner. On March 31, the day before the official start of the implementation of the Settlement Plan, South African Foreign Minister Botha informed Special Representative Ahtisaari that armed SWAPO guerrillas had infiltrated Namibian territory from Angola. Over the next three days, more than 1,000 SWAPO fighters crossed the border. In a letter to UN Secretary-General Perez de Cuellar, Botha threatened to abort the transition process if the UN refused to authorize deployment of South African military forces. British Prime Minister Margaret Thatcher, who was visiting the region at the time, supported South African redeployment, arguing that the UN's credibility was at stake. Prime Minister Thatcher, however, also warned Botha that the international community would react harshly if South Africa refused to abide by the terms of Resolution 435.

Ahtisaari was faced with what one UNTAG official called a "savage dilemma." He recognized that if South African forces were permitted to respond, there was a serious possibility that the entire peace process could unravel. At the same time, Ahtisaari believed that the SWAPO incursion also posed a threat to the overall transition process and that he had little choice but to release South African troops for the purpose of countering the apparent infiltration. With the arrival of peacekeeping troops delayed by the budget debate in New York, Ahtisaari had few troops or support personnel at his disposal. In any event, UNTAG could not engage SWAPO forces and would have been powerless, even if fully deployed, to prevent South African troops from leaving their bases.

In view of the circumstances, Ahtisaari authorized South Africa on April 1 to redeploy a specified number of forces from the bases to which they had been confined. Territorial authorities also reconstituted Koevoet units in SWAPOL. Violent clashes ensued, and approximately 300 PLAN fighters and up to 30 territorial police and South African soldiers were killed, a higher number of casualties than in any single battle during the 23 years of war. Human rights groups and journalists accused the South African security forces of ruthless search-and-destroy missions against fleeing PLAN fighters, and newspapers in South Africa and Europe reported that some fighters had been shot at close range rather than killed as a result of confrontations in the bush. The AG, however, would later call Koevoet the "saviors of democracy."

SWAPO subsequently criticized the South African claim of an incursion, calling it a ploy "to derail the transition process" and "to undermine SWAPO's popularity at home and international support abroad." SWAPO officials denied that PLAN members had crossed the border from Angola. They asserted that the fighting involved guerrillas already based in northern Namibia who were reporting to UN checkpoints for confinement to bases under UN supervision, and they sharply criticized Ahtisaari for permitting the South African forces to leave the bases to which they had been confined. Later, without addressing further the issue of whether the PLAN fighters crossed the border, SWAPO emphasized that the fighters South Africa discovered in Namibia lacked any hostile intent.

South Africa and many Western countries maintained that a SWAPO incursion was a violation of Resolution 435 and the 1988 Geneva Protocol. The Geneva Protocol of August 1988 stated that Angola and Cuba would use their "good offices" to ensure that "once the total withdrawal of South African troops from Angola is completed, and within the context also of the cessation of hostilities in Namibia, SWAPO's forces will be deployed to the north of the 16th parallel." However, because SWAPO was kept out of the negotiation process from the time Resolution 435 was adopted, it was not a party to the Geneva Protocol and actually never committed to keep its troops north of the 16th parallel. A letter written by SWAPO President Nujoma to the Secretary-General on August 12 committed SWAPO "to take the necessary steps to help make the peace process...irreversible and successful" and "to comply with the commencement of the cessation of hostile acts." This letter was interpreted by Western diplomats to commit SWAPO to the Geneva Protocol, but it actually only indicated that SWAPO would comply with the ceasefire already agreed to in Resolution 435.

At the same time, SWAPO certainly knew that the regional peace accords were intended to prohibit SWAPO guerrillas from entering the territory. Consequently, there has been considerable speculation concerning the motivation behind the organization's decision to challenge the accords. The location of SWAPO bases inside Namibia had been a major bone of contention during the negotiations in 1977 and 1978, and it had prompted the ultimately fruitless negotiations over the establishment of a demilitarized zone. SWAPO had long wanted to interpret the Settlement Plan to authorize the confinement to base of PLAN members already inside the territory, but not stationed at military bases *per se*. By sending troops into the country, SWAPO may well have been attempting to make its open military presence inside the country a *fait accompli*. Such a presence could have potentially increased SWAPO's domestic prestige as a liberating organization. In addition, some observers also speculate that SWAPO may have seen its action as a way of demonstrating the necessity for UNTAG to deploy a larger military force.

With the United States, the Soviet Union and UNTAG acting as observers, the Joint Commission met in emergency session at the Mt. Etjo game ranch outside Windhoek on April 8 and 9. After SWAPO declared a willingness to withdraw its forces, the parties issued the Mt. Etjo Declaration on April 9. Reaffirming the parties' commitment to the tripartite accord, the Mt. Etjo Declaration called for the restoration of the ceasefire and provided for the withdrawal of SWAPO troops to Angola to points north of the 16th parallel, about 100 miles north of the border. With some reluctance, SWAPO combatants eventually reported to designated sites and were escorted to Angola. SADF was not fully confined to base until May 13. Thus, from the outset the implementation process was six weeks behind schedule.

Chapter 4

DEVELOPMENT OF LEGAL FRAMEWORK FOR ELECTIONS

Key to Resolution 435's success was the development of a free and fair election process that would provide Namibians an opportunity to choose representatives who would draft a constitution for an independent Namibia. The Settlement Plan specified certain prerequisites for a free and fair election in the Namibian context: universal suffrage for all adult Namibians, including those who could not read and write; a secret ballot; participation as a voter, candidate or party activist free from intimidation; an adequate campaign period; and guarantees of full freedom of speech, assembly, movement and press. Subsequent agreements, formal and informal, specified aspects of the electoral system in more detail.

Despite prior agreement between the AG and the SR on fundamental issues, the process of developing the legal framework for the election process produced protracted negotiations. Although the Settlement Plan left responsibility for the conduct of the election in the hands of the Administrator-General, the requirement that the Special Representative be satisfied at each stage gave the SR substantial power over the substance of election-related legislation. Indeed, at several points in the negotiating process, the AG's refusal to agree to the SR's demands on proposed legislation almost brought the 435 process to a halt.

Three groups of laws had to be adopted before the electoral process could meet the conditions set forth in the Settlement Plan and the subsequent agreements: 1) laws ensuring that an environment existed in which all Namibians could participate in the process in a meaningful manner; 2) laws establishing an administratively effective and fair election system; and 3) a law establishing the Constituent Assembly. In each case, the AG presented legislation to the SR. With respect to the laws governing the registration and electoral processes and the Constituent Assembly, the AG also made the proposed laws public and solicited comments. The AG received extensive comments from interested parties, both domestic and international, and the SR subsequently pursued many of these comments in negotiations with the AG. Repeatedly, as negotiations stalled, the SR referred issues to Pretoria through senior South African officials in Namibia or through the South African ambassador to the UN in New York. The negotiations eventually concluded with agreement on the terms of the legislation and an "exchange of letters" between the AG and SR setting forth supplementary decisions regarding the law and the administrative process.

Creating an Environment for Free and Fair Elections

Prior to the implementation of Resolution 435, Namibian law included various statutes that discriminated against the non-white population. Because it would be impossible to hold truly free elections with such laws in effect, the Settlement Plan called for the repeal of all "discriminatory or restrictive laws, regulations, or administrative measures which might abridge or inhibit" the holding of free and fair elections. Similarly, an environment had to be created in which individuals did not fear arrest and detention based on past or present political activities. This point particularly concerned the many Namibians who had left the territory and had engaged in activities that, absent new protections, might have led to criminal charges. To deal with this situation, the Settlement Plan called for the Administrator-General to release "all Namibian political prisoners or political detainees" and to permit "[a]ll Namibian refugees or Namibians detained or otherwise outside the territory...to return peacefully" so that both groups could "participate fully and freely in the electoral process without risk of arrest, detention, intimidation or imprisonment."

Legislation covering amnesty and the repeal of discriminatory laws was not promulgated until June 6, more than two months after the beginning of implementation. In April, the AG initially proposed an amnesty that the SR considered inadequate because it would have permitted subsequent prosecution of returnees for common crimes. The AG also resisted repealing a number of discriminatory laws, evidently because, in his view, the Settlement Plan required only the repeal of laws that would inhibit free and fair elections, not laws designed to protect the security of the state.

After considerable negotiation involving the South African ambassador to the UN and the foreign minister in Pretoria, the AG and the SR reached agreement on the amnesty and discriminatory laws. With the publication of Proclamations AG 13 (amnesty) and AG 14 (repeal of discriminatory laws) in the *Official Gazette* on June 12, the UNHCR began the repatriation of Namibians in exile, and the transition proceeded.

Proclamation AG 13, the amnesty proclamation, provided that no criminal proceedings could be instituted against any Namibian who returned to Namibia after living outside the territory. To be eligible for the amnesty, though, a person had to return through one of six designated entry points and receive an official document attesting to that fact.

Proclamation AG 14 repealed 36 pieces of legislation and substantially amended 10 others. The proclamation repealed various territorial and South African laws applicable in the territory, especially those governing "internal security." These included laws that: authorized the suppression of political dissent under the guise of "communism"; banned or otherwise restricted political organizations; suspended legal rights in the context of a state of emergency; authorized detention without trial; and imposed a curfew throughout much of the territory. The proclamation also ended conscription of Namibians and removed the power of the South African president to terminate trials of security personnel.

In addition, the proclamation provided that interested parties could petition the AG for repeal or amendment of additional laws that were believed to inhibit free and fair elections; a response by the AG was required within 21 days. This comment period provided a basis for the SR to approve the proclamation, even though he did not view it as completely inclusive.

The most objectionable outstanding law was Proclamation AG 8 of 1980, which established the ethnic administration system in Namibia. Although the SR pushed for AG 8's repeal, the AG resisted overthrowing this law, arguing that it did not relate to the election process. In an October 1989 report, the Secretary-General continued to insist that AG 8 violated "the spirit, if not the letter, of the Settlement Plan," and Security Council Resolution 643 of October 31, 1989 expressly endorsed the position of the Secretary-General that "AG 8 should be repealed."

Election System

A major challenge of the Settlement Plan was the adoption of an effective and efficient election system that took into account geographic and demographic considerations. Both the AG and the SR interpreted the Settlement Plan to mean that the laws governing the election process were South Africa's to write. Accordingly, the AG assumed responsibility for presenting an initial proposal.

Not surprisingly, the Administrator-General's proposals were based on the system used for the 1978 internal elections. This system called for a highly centralized election process that was cumbersome and complex. In addition, according to observers from the Namibian Council of Churches, the 1978 elections had been marred by administrative fraud, which permitted significant numbers of non-Namibians to vote.

The AG's proposed system faced immediate and considerable criticism. The NDI delegation that visited Namibia in May and June concluded that the "election system currently being devised by the Administrator-General is overly centralized, deprives political parties an opportunity to scrutinize all aspects of the balloting process and does not provide for a speedy tabulation of the results." Other governmental and nongovernmental observers echoed these criticisms. Ultimately, at the insistence of the SR, the AG altered his initial proposal and adopted a decentralized system that met recognized international standards. Nonetheless, the delay in adopting the electoral system, for a time, appeared to endanger the overall transition process.

Voter Registration Law

The election system was based, in the first instance, on the premise that a separate registration process to determine voter eligibility would best guarantee the integrity of the elections. In addition to identifying prospective voters, the voter registration program also provided election administrators an opportunity to train local election officials, to become familiar with residential patterns, and to educate prospective voters.

The AG issued a draft voter registration law on April 24, 1989. Under the draft, a chief registration officer would administer the entire registration process with the assistance of 23 district supervisors. Registration would be open to anyone 18 years of age or older, who was born in Namibia, had at least one parent who was born in Namibia, or had lived in the territory for at least four years.

Before the close of the comment period, some 70 political parties, religious groups, human rights organizations and individuals formally filed comments. Critics expressed concern about individuals who might attempt to circumvent the process by registering without any intention of becoming a Namibian citizen. There was particular concern that South African civil servants would register, as well as Angolans, Hereros from Botswana and citizens from the Republic of South Africa, and that these groups would then vote for the more pro-South African parties.

Critics faulted the system for not providing a voter registration roll; the chief registration officer would be under no obligation to publish any registration list, making specific registration challenges difficult. To accommodate migrant workers, the proposed law did not require voters to register where they lived, which precluded a local registration roll. There also was substantial concern about the production and distribution of bogus identification documents.

Because the Settlement Plan had postponed the issue of the status of Walvis Bay, Walvis Bay residents could not register and vote unless they were otherwise eligible (i.e., they were born in Namibia or of Namibian parents). These qualified individuals had to register and cast their ballots in Swakopmund, just across the Walvis Bay border.

After extensive negotiations, the Special Representative and the Administrator-General agreed to important changes in the registration law: government civil servants would have to declare an intention to stay in Namibia before they would be permitted to register, and the government would publish a weekly list of registered voters in the *Official Gazette*. Regarding identification, the SR and AG agreed that all applicants who based their eligibility on the four-year residency requirement had to provide accompanying documentary evidence. Returnees repatriated by the United Nations High Commissioner for Refugees who were natural children of persons born in Namibia, however, needed only to swear to that fact rather than provide documentary evidence. Natural children not sponsored by the UNHCR had to produce such documentary evidence of age and parentage. Individuals without identity documents were permitted to register by means of a written declaration if they were identified by a bona fide registered voter or by a traditional chief or headman. In deciding cases where individuals lacked proper identification, registration officers had the discretion to make age determinations.

The SR and the AG agreed that registration officials could not deny an application for registration without the concurrence of a local UNTAG official. This important principle, which placed UNTAG officials directly in the decision-making process, was known at the UN as the "6(e) principle," after the paragraph in the exchange of letters that established it. These letters further specified that when the AG and UNTAG officials could not agree, the matter would be presented to the AG and UNTAG counterparts at the next higher level of authority.

The registration law was made official by its publication in the *Official Gazette* on June 30, 1989, and the AG and SR exchanged letters, which were published in the *Official Gazette* on July 1. Registration began on July 3.

By accepting the finalized voter registration law, the Special Representative accepted the basic design of a centrally-controlled election system. Indeed, as the registration period began, the AG's election division had completed a very detailed plan for the entire election procedure, while the SR appeared to be taking "one step at a time."

Registration of Parties Law

Due to prolonged delays in negotiating the election law, the AG and SR agreed in August to incorporate into a separate law the provisions regarding the eligibility and registration of parties. This enabled the parties to register and the campaign to proceed without a final agreement on the electoral system.

The law governing registration of political organizations was made public on September 4. It provided for the appointment of a chief electoral officer and established the procedures for parties to register by filing an application with a registration court. To qualify for the election, a party had to file its name, abbreviation and proposed symbol along with at least 2,000 signatures of registered voters and a deposit of R10,000 (about $4,000). The court would review the application and recommend to the AG whether the application met the criteria. Under the terms of an exchange of letters, the AG undertook to obtain the prior concurrence of the SR before rejecting the application of a prospective party.

Election Law

One of the most serious disputes between the Administrator-General and the Special Representative centered on the law establishing the election system. Negotiations over the law produced a stalemate for much of the summer and delayed the promulgation of the final law until less than a month before the election.

The AG proposed an election law on July 21 and requested comments within 21 days. The proposed law, which governed voting and ballot counting, was based on the 1978 framework. It was familiar to several UNTAG election officials who, in the 1980s, had reviewed the 1978 law in preparation for implementation. Some of those UN officials recalled telling the South Africans that a system based on the 1978 scheme would be totally unacceptable.

The AG's draft called for an election based on a nationwide proportional representation system for 72 at-large seats, with each voter casting a ballot for a political party preference of his or her choice. The law established a centralized system to verify a voter's identification and to count ballots. It also created a complicated numbered ballot system purportedly designed to prevent the counting of ineligible votes; only after all registration cards and ballots had been sent to Windhoek, and officials verified each voter's signature or thumbprint, would the ballots be counted.

The international community found the proposed system unacceptable in several respects. First, enclosing ballots in numbered envelopes corresponding to numbers on the voters' identification cards compromised ballot secrecy. Second, the proposed centralized verification and counting process departed from the internationally recognized practice of counting votes locally and, according to the AG's election officials, would have taken approximately two to six weeks to complete. Third, the proposed system denied political parties access to the polling stations. Finally, the draft allowed government civil servants to act as electoral officials when assisting illiterate and handicapped voters in marking ballots, which some saw as creating the potential for official manipulation.

In justifying these measures, the AG stressed that for most of the population this was their first election experience and that the local election administrators lacked the background necessary to guard against fraud. He also argued that barring party representatives from the polling sites was necessary to ensure the efficient operation of the process and to avoid voter intimidation. The international community, however, viewed these arguments as specious, and the battle over the appropriate election system was joined.

The NDI delegation that visited Namibia in May and June identified several areas where modifications to the election law would be desirable. Specifically, the delegation recommended: an independent election commission; subdivision of the 23 electoral districts into smaller units; an absentee ballot procedure for those voters not in their district on election day; verification of a voter's identity at the polling site, with "tendered ballots" used in cases of challenges; elimination of the use of numbered ballots; an extensive voter education program to ensure that the population understood the voting procedures; access of party representatives to the polling sites; and tabulation of ballots at district counting centers. In a meeting with the NDI delegation at the end of the visit, the SR seemingly accepted the merits of the delegation's recommendations, except for an independent election commission, which he believed would remove the AG from responsibility for the conduct of the elections in contradiction of the Settlement Plan's mandate.

Nonetheless, by late July, the Special Representative appeared ready to endorse the AG's basic framework, provided that it guaranteed ballot secrecy. Ahtisaari thought the basic structure was sound, and he was not concerned about substantial variations in electoral procedures that stemmed from cultural differences. Further, he did not believe it was his role to tamper with the administrative procedures or force a quicker count. These matters under discussion were not sufficiently important, in Ahtisaari's view, to jeopardize the schedule for the transition. Finally, Ahtisaari may have minimized the significance of the fact that the international community, which did not trust the South Africans, considered the centralized verification and counting system as being subject to manipulation.

Eventually, though, the international pressure to modify the draft law became overwhelming. Questions relating to the mechanics of the system dominated a hearing in July before the African Subcommittee of the U.S. Congress, with bipartisan consensus that the proposed system was unacceptable. The Commonwealth nations, meeting in Malaysia in August, adopted a resolution calling for amendments to the election law. Finally, on August 29, 1989, the Security Council adopted Resolution 640, which demanded "strict compliance by all parties concerned, especially South Africa, with the terms of resolutions 435 (1978) and 632 (1989)" and which requested the Secretary-General "ensure that all legislation concerning the electoral process is in conformity with the provisions of the Settlement Plan" and with "internationally accepted norms for free and fair elections." Accordingly, the SR recognized that, whatever the merits of South Africa's proposed system under local conditions, the process had to meet international standards.

In this context, the Secretary-General sent Paul Szasz, a recently retired UN lawyer, to Windhoek in August to assist with the negotiations. The negotiations dragged on through August and September; from time to time they appeared about to break off altogether. Agreement was finally reached on October 6, and the AG published the final election law in the *Official Gazette* a week later, only 25 days before balloting was scheduled to begin.

The final election law incorporated virtually all of the changes that had been suggested. These included:

- eliminating the use of numbered envelopes;

- centralizing verification and counting (the tendered ballot process required only in those cases where the voter's identification was in question) with most ballots being counted in the 23 district centers;

- permitting persons outside of the districts in which they registered to vote by tendered ballot;

- requiring that an UNTAG supervisor be present whenever an election administrator explained the ballot marking process;

- providing political party representatives access to all polling stations and counting centers; and

- requiring that even illiterate voters mark their ballots alone in the voting booth.

The exchange of letters between the SR and the AG once again ensured that UNTAG supervisors would retain an active role in the administration of the balloting process, particularly on questions about voter eligibility or decisions requiring closing the poll. The AG also committed to appoint as election officers persons of "integrity" who met other specified criteria, and the SR retained the right to approve these appointments. Finally, in accordance with Resolution 435, the AG agreed to obtain the consent of the SR before announcing the official results of the election and the allocation of seats in the Constituent Assembly.

Constituent Assembly Law

The AG presented a draft law governing the Constituent Assembly in August. Under the proposed version, the AG could control the procedures of the Constituent Assembly and the substance of the constitution. It also incorporated the constitutional principles adopted to in 1982 and made them binding on the assembly, but in reducing the principles to specific language, certain subtle changes were made. In addition, the draft law gave the South African-appointed territorial courts the power to review the constitution and the actions of the assembly. The proposed law would also have required each member of the assembly to swear before a South African judge, and it designated the AG or his nominee as President Pro Tem of the assembly. Most significantly, the assembly could only "recommend" initiatives to the AG and he would be under no obligation to implement them; in effect, he would have a veto over any provision in the new constitution.

The draft proclamation represented such a difference of perception and approach between the AG and SR that the SR decided against entering into negotiations until the election law negotiations were settled. The strategy was to avoid further complicating the negotiations over the election law and avert the possibility of tradeoffs between the two laws. The Security Council, in Resolution 640, charged the Secretary-General with the responsibility to ensure that the proclamation on the Constituent Assembly "respects the sovereign will of the people of Namibia."

The idea that the assembly could only make recommendations to the AG was never considered as a serious proposal, and the AG backed down. More problematic were the issues of incorporating the 1982 constitutional principles and the possibility of enforcement by judicial review. SWAPO and UNTAG argued that South Africa should not be in a position to dictate the terms of the constitution for an independent and sovereign Namibia, and that the actions of the assembly should not be subject to the jurisdiction of the South African-appointed courts. The other political parties and the AG argued that the principles had been incorporated into the Settlement Plan and agreed to by SWAPO in 1982, and that only by including them in the empowering proclamation could they be made binding and enforceable. They criticized SWAPO's argument that the principles should not be forced upon the assembly by the South Africans or the Contact Group, because the same argument could be made about the entire process, and they argued that judicial review of the constitution and the assembly was the only practical way to enforce the 1982 agreement. The parties criticized UNTAG for its alleged partiality in agreeing with SWAPO on this matter.

The Special Representative sought a law that would secure an independently functioning assembly and would establish the basic procedural guidelines for the assembly. Nothing in the law, the SR argued, should govern the content of the constitution. He took the position that the assembly derived its authority from the elections, not from South African law, and that the 1982 principles were governed by international law that had to be immune from local law.

For a time, negotiations over the Constituent Assembly law broke down. The SR was prepared to permit the elections to occur without any Constituent Assembly law, in which case the assembly would have been responsible for adopting its own procedures.

Ultimately the SR's position prevailed, and the AG promulgated the law on November 6, 1989, one day before the elections began. The law provided that the assembly have four functions: 1) to draw up a constitution and to adopt it by a two-thirds majority; 2) to determine a date for independence; 3) to declare formally that independence; and 4) to form a government, subject to the constitution. All that remained of the AG's grab for dominance was a provision that the assembly "seek the views of the Administrator-General" before it determined the date for independence. With the Constituent Assembly law in place, the election proceeded and political debate over the issue ceased. The law became the legal framework for the proceedings of the Constituent Assembly, which commenced on November 15.

Chapter 5

PREPARING FOR ELECTIONS

Repatriation of Exiled Namibians

During 23 years of war, thousands of Namibians left their homes to live in exile. Most lived in refugee camps in neighboring Angola and Zambia. The Settlement Plan provided that, after the declaration of a general amnesty, all Namibians living outside the territory be given an opportunity to return. Because it took until June 12 for the SR and the AG to negotiate the final laws granting amnesty and repealing discriminatory laws, the UN High Commissioner for Refugees (UNHCR) could not begin the repatriation process until after that date.

Before the transition, the UN had been providing a stipend through SWAPO to assist an estimated 68,400 refugees, and accordingly the UNHCR planned for as many as 69,000 returnees. The actual number repatriated turned out to be significantly smaller.

The UNHCR repatriated about 42,000 Namibians mostly between June and September, from Angola, Zambia and more than 40 other countries. The UNHCR office in Namibia, headed by Nicholas Bwakira, provided transportation to six designated entry points, three each for those returning by air and by land. With the assistance of the Namibian Council of Churches (CCN), the UNHCR operated five reception centers in central and northern Namibia. Upon arrival at reception centers, returnees received material assistance and help with resettlement plans. Upon their departure, the UNHCR supplied a month's food rations and other assistance, and the UN World Food Program provided additional assistance.

The reception centers were intended to provide only temporary refuge. They typically were located in large fields and resembled military encampments. Long rows of large green tents able to sleep six filled the field, and there were communal outdoor shower and bathroom facilities.

Returnees were supposed to stay no longer than seven days at reception centers, but some refused to leave and others had difficulty locating family members or finding places to resettle. At the Dobra center, outside Windhoek, large numbers of people refused to leave ostensibly because they feared reprisals and intimidation by the security forces in the north. This center, which had a maximum capacity of 2,000, housed almost 2,600 returnees during the peak of the process. SWAPO was accused of persuading returnees to stay at Dobra, so that they could be mobilized for political purposes in the campaign.

At the Kavango reception center, four returnees who had left to resettle in the community subsequently returned, citing fears for their safety. In fact, no actual cases of assault or violence against resettled persons were reported, but the concerns led to overcrowding at times. Many individuals, unable or unwilling to resettle into the community, were sent to secondary reception centers sponsored by the CCN, although these centers were primarily intended for the elderly, orphans and pregnant women.

In general, Namibian society absorbed the returnees quickly. The process was nearly complete by early August, and by September 29, all but 579 returnees had resettled in their former communities.

The most prominent returnee was Sam Nujoma, the president of SWAPO, who had lived in exile since 1960. On September 14, Nujoma returned on a special flight from Luanda and was greeted with a jubilant welcome. His return, which received broad international media coverage, marked the beginning of a new stage in Namibian history.

Political Prisoners

Government Political Prisoners

The Settlement Plan required South African authorities to release all political prisoners inside Namibia, and it called for any disputes concerning political prisoners to be resolved to the satisfaction of the Special Representative, acting on the advice of a "jurist of international standing." The independent jurist, Carl Norgaard of Denmark, examined the cases of convicted prisoners and others awaiting trial to determine whether these persons had been imprisoned for political reasons and therefore eligible for release.

On July 20, the AG announced the release of 25 political prisoners, 23 of whom were released immediately. Human rights organizations identified eight persons not released by the AG as political prisoners. Although stating that a few cases were still pending, the SR expressed atisfaction that the initial group of prisoners had been released.

SWAPO Detainees

During the transition, allegations that SWAPO continued to detain political prisoners developed into a major controversy. In April and May, the International Society for Human Rights, Amnesty International and the SWAPO-Democrats, a small anti-SWAPO party, informed the Special Representative of the names of some 260 persons allegedly held by SWAPO. SWAPO acknowledged that it had arrested and imprisoned Namibians accused of spying for South Africa during the war, but denied that it continued to hold anyone. In late May, however, SWAPO released about 200 detainees from a camp near Lubango, Angola, and in July SWAPO released a second group of 84. The UNHCR returned a total of 232 ex-detainees on special flights on July 4, July 29 and August 8.

Some of those released told of torture and murder in refugee camps. As the ex-detainees began to return, two organizations of ex-detainees and their relatives, the Parents' Committee and the Political Consultative Council, issued lists containing the names of hundreds of additional persons allegedly still detained in SWAPO camps in Angola and Zambia. These groups called on the UN to investigate. Church and human rights organizations also argued that SWAPO should be fully accountable for its political prisoners.

SWAPO ignored the charges of mistreatment or shrugged them off as a logical consequence of war. In a press conference on August 23, SWAPO Foreign Affairs Secretary Theo-Ben Gurirab admitted that SWAPO had detained people on espionage charges, including some who turned out to be innocent. With the return of the ex-detainees to Namibia, it became clear that certain SWAPO officials had taken the law into their own hands and had acted brutally toward the prisoners. Gurirab publicly expressed regret over this conduct and promised to bring to justice the guilty individuals. In the same press conference, SWAPO Secretary for Information Hidipo Hamutenya reiterated the organization's assertion that all people who had been detained on espionage charges had been released. He invited the International Committee of the Red Cross (ICRC), Amnesty International and the UNHCR to form an independent delegation to travel to Angola and Zambia, with the permission of those governments, to inspect the camps for alleged detainees.

The Settlement Plan expressly required the Special Representative to be satisfied that all Namibians remaining outside of the territory did so freely and voluntarily. UNTAG officials eventually compiled a consolidated list of 1,100 names of persons allegedly detained.

After some difficulty obtaining permission from the Angolan and Zambian governments, a UN investigatory delegation comprised of UNTAG and UNHCR officials traveled to both countries from September 2 to 21 for the purpose of visiting 16 identified SWAPO camps where political prisoners were allegely still being held. One UNTAG official involved in the mission later commented: "we went there with the intention that we would come back with a clear record for SWAPO." Despite requests by the SR, the ICRC, citing its limited mandate, declined to participate in the mission and UNTAG refused to include any former detainees.

SWAPO assisted the delegation's visits to refugee camps, hospitals, schools, prisons and other facilities. The delegation visited 15 of 16 camps named by the ex-detainees, missing one only because of nearby hostilities stemming from the Angolan war. The investigation uncovered no evidence that SWAPO was continuing to hold prisoners and identified no former detainees who were being prevented from returning home.

On October 16, the mission released its report. After accounting for 110 duplicated entries, the report separated the remaining names on its consolidated list as follows: 1) 484 persons released and/or repatriated; 2) 71 persons reportedly not detained, including SWAPO officials; 3) 115 persons reported dead; 4) 52 persons unidentified because of insufficient information; and 5) 315 persons whose status was unknown. By November, UNTAG had reduced the number of alleged detainees still unaccounted for to 263.

The report carefully described the logistical and information obstacles confronting the mission. Nevertheless, with the mission unable to locate any detainees, and with no second party corroboration, SWAPO political opponents and former detainees labeled the mission a whitewash and characterized it as one more example of UN partiality. In fact, many SWAPO opponents made the allegations of continuing detentions a focal point of their campaigns, arguably exploiting the issue for political gain.

Registration of Voters

Voter registration began on July 3. Some 110 mobile registration units complemented the 36 fixed registration centers and 35 temporary locations throughout the 23 electoral districts. A total of 230 UNTAG supervisors, together with interpreters and CIVPOL monitors, participated in the registration process.

For each eligible individual, officials completed a registration card in duplicate. One copy was issued to the voter and a second was sent to the Central Register in Windhoek. An UNTAG computer expert and team of officials supervised the compilation of the Central Register. As required by the law, authorities published a list of registered voters by district and in alphabetical order on a weekly basis in the *Official Gazette*.

When registration began, the AG directed government civil servants to serve as official registrars, but two weeks later his office announced that the assignments were temporary and that the personnel would rotate. This constant turnover also slowed the process.

The South West African Broadcast Company (SWABC) broadcast schedules for mobile units throughout the country. In the north, though, registration officials unfamiliar with the terrain often miscalculated travel times for mobile units. Therefore the scheduled broadcast and the actual arrival times were inconsistent. In many instances, mobile units would arrive at a scheduled destination to find no one there, and conversely people would appear at scheduled times, some traveling great distances, only to wait in vain for a registration team.

SWAPO expressed concerns, echoed by various observer groups, that the registration teams missed significant numbers of people. These organizations claimed that registration points were spaced too far apart; that mobile teams stopped too close to tribal offices, police stations and ex-Koevoet bases; that registration sites were consistently closed; and that mobile teams often departed before allowing everyone an opportunity to register. Critics also complained of chronic communication problems among registration officials, inadequate supplies of registration materials, and lack of uniformity in the preparation of registration cards. SWAPO and others also believed that substantial numbers of DTA sympathizers from Angola and Zambia registering in the north, and they objected to the fact that various organizations in South Africa were funding the transportation of eligible South Africans to register.

Despite these problems, when registration ended on September 23 -- one week later than originally scheduled in order to give all eligible individuals a chance to register -- a total of 701,483 potential voters had registered, a number greater than the estimated number of the eligible population. The registration, in fact, amounted to a census of the population; villages, of which authorities had been unaware, were uncovered by mobile units and placed on the map. Only 593 applications were rejected, in each case with the concurrence of an UNTAG supervisor.

The intense interest of the Namibian people in the election process became particularly evident during the registration process. One UNTAG official related the story of a man in his 60's who walked some 10 kilometers from his village to a mobile registration center. The man told officials that his very elderly father wanted to register but was unable to walk, and he asked if they could go to his village. When the response was noncommittal, the man left. He returned hours later with his father, having carried the old man the entire way.

Registration of Parties

Eleven parties submitted applications to the registration court by the date of its first sitting on September 12. The court determined that nine parties qualified for registration under the law. It gave two other parties, the Namibia Christian Democratic Party and the Christian Democratic Action for Social Justice, an additional two weeks to obtain the necessary signatures. The latter party subsequently obtained the requisite signatures, and thus a total of 10 parties qualified to participate in the election.

Chapter 6
POLITICAL ENVIRONMENT

Problem of Intimidation

Throughout most of the campaign period, charges and counter-charges of intimidation dominated the political agenda. For a time, the extent of intimidation threatened to jeopardize a free election altogether. Problems of intimidation ranged from relatively minor incidents of excessive partisan enthusiasm to killings, and included at least one case of a politically motivated assassination. They also involved assaults by current and former members of Koevoet, acts and threats of serious violence, implied threats from employers, strikes by students and teachers, and many ominous but unfounded rumors.

Koevoet

The Koevoet counterinsurgency force posed perhaps the single greatest menace to free and fair elections. Koevoet members were responsible for many incidents of intimidation, and their continued presence within SWAPOL forces undermined public confidence generally in the transition process.

Although the Settlement Plan charged the transition government with "primary responsibility for maintaining law and order" through the "existing police forces," it also required South African authorities to disband "the citizen forces, commandos and ethnic forces." This provision clearly required the demobilization of Koevoet and the SWATF, even though these forces were created after the development of the Settlement Plan itself. (The 1982 agreement on impartiality expressly mentioned SWATF.) In response to the SWAPO incursion in April, the AG remobilized Koevoet members, who ended up leading the brutal response. Although Koevoet was technically disbanded in May, at least

1,200 former members of the Koevoet force were simply transferred into SWAPOL, the territorial police. As part of SWAPOL, Koevoet units continued to operate intact under the command of Major General Dreyer, who directed all SWAPOL units in the north. Koevoet units in SWAPOL also continued to use armored personnel carriers known as "casspirs." This vehicle is the size of a large dump truck, with a V-shaped underside to deflect mine blasts. In the early months of the transition, casspirs patrolled the territory equipped with machine guns mounted on their roofs, a clear violation of the Settlement Plan's authorization for the police to carry only "small arms." In June, following protests by international observers including NDI, UNTAG pressured SWAPOL to discontinue this practice, although it was reported that security personnel still carried heavy arms inside the vehicles. SWAPOL units used casspirs even for routine appearances, such as to patrol peaceful political rallies. In their defense, SWAPOL personnel explained that they feared patrolling in anything less than casspirs, because of local animosity towards the territorial police force.

CIVPOL's efforts to monitor the casspir patrols were hampered by a shortage of mine-resistent vehicles, a problem exacerbated by SWAPOL's lack of cooperation. In the north, SWAPOL casspir patrols often intentionally eluded the slower, less numerous CIVPOL vehicles. Accordingly, UNTAG sought to acquire its own casspirs to use on CIVPOL patrols. One SWAPO official, however, questioned whether merely painting these vehicles white for UNTAG's use would be enough to erase the taint and negative symbolism attached to casspirs by the local population. In any event, in September, UNTAG finally obtained approximately 27 mine-resistant vehicles including casspirs.

Resolution 640, adopted in August, demanded the demobilization of Koevoet. At the insistence of UNTAG, territorial authorities finally dismissed about 1,200 former members of Koevoet from SWAPOL in late September.

The DTA recruited former Koevoet members to participate in the party's campaign activities. After the demobilization of Koevoet, most complaints of intimidation were directed at political partisans, many of whom were former Koevoet members working as DTA organizers or wearing DTA colors.

Partisan Violence

Politically motivated intimidation on both sides led to significant violence. During a single week in August, for example, a 10-year-old girl was reported shot in the face with an arrow at a SWAPO march in Oshakati; six teachers were reportedly admitted to a hospital in Oshikuku with minor injuries after DTA partisans allegedly attacked them with whips known as sjamboks; and a convoy of DTA supporters allegedly drove through the Engela reception center firing shots. In September, DTA supporters marched through Katutura, the black township outside Windhoek, throwing stones at houses with SWAPO colors. A former Koevoet member who subsequently joined SWAPO was killed, allegedly by other former Koevoet members.

In the north, specific incidents occurred during the weekends of September 30, after the demobilization of Koevoet, and October 7, following a massive rally marking Sam Nujoma's first visit to Ovamboland since his return to Namibia. Over the latter weekend, three people were killed and more than 30 were injured. Two of the dead were killed by a hand grenade thrown from a moving car into a crowd of SWAPO supporters, and 21 people were injured by explosions of grenades and tear gas during an attack on a school in Ongwediva.

The most notable political assassination was the September 12 murder of Anton Lubowski, SWAPO's Deputy Election Director and its highest ranking white member. Local authorities arrested an Irish national in connection with the killing, and reports in the international press implicated members of the South African police in the crime. In addition, in August and September, anonymous death threats were directed at David Smuts, a leading human rights lawyer, Gwen Lister, the editor of *The Namibian,* John Liebenberg, a politically active photographer, and UNTAG officials.

Allegations of intimidation were also directed at SWAPO supporters. Tribal headmen and chiefs who had cooperated with the South African government in administering the homelands feared retaliation by repatriated SWAPO members. In May, 11 headmen led by Gabriel Kautuima, senior headman and leader of the Kwanyama tribe of Ovambo, obtained a court order that required the Commissioner of Police to "make the necessary arrangements to protect the lives and property of the headmen." An NDI-sponsored delegation, which visited Chief Kautuima that month, noted that his house was riddled with bullet holes. In June, a group of 22 headmen including Kautuima petitioned the Special Representative and the Administrator-General, *inter alia*, to force SWAPO to cease "all forms of violence, intimidation and false propaganda" and to request that "SWAPO be prevented from taking part in the election."

Headmen were not alone in raising accusations against SWAPO partisans. One DTA official accused SWAPO supporters of murdering a DTA organizer and of ambushing a bus of DTA supporters returning to Ovamboland from an August rally in Windhoek.

UNTAG officials throughout the country were also harassed and threatened. On August 18, assailants attacked an UNTAG district office in Outijo, killing an UNTAG security guard. The actual extent of serious intimidation, especially during the last weeks before the election, was difficult to gauge. Many reported instances may have consisted of excessive partisan enthusiasm, such as relatively benign forms of jeering and harassment. At the same time, intimidation remained the most serious threat to the realization of free and fair elections.

Employer Pressures

Many white farmers were reluctant to allow SWAPO partisans onto their property to talk with farm workers, but UNTAG insisted that this access be allowed. Many employers also attempted to influence directly the voting decisions of their employees. In Tsumeb, for example, a construction company fired five SWAPO supporters for failing to attend a DTA meeting. UNTAG officials successfully negotiated a tentative agreement with the company to rehire the employees, but the company reneged on the agreement when the incident received publicity in *The Namibian*. More subtly, many white farmers transported their black employees to the polls in trucks decorated in DTA colors.

School Boycotts

The Namibia National Student Organization (NANSO) organized a mass boycott of classes in April to demonstrate against the continued presence of Koevoet forces in the north. Ovambo teachers joined the strike on May 27. The AG charged NANSO with political intimidation, by accusing NANSO members of coercing students and teachers into participating. The AG threatened to bar students from school unless they re-registered and agreed to refrain from political activity. The boycotts were terminated on June 20, but sporadic strikes continued throughout the summer.

Rumors and Threats

Throughout the campaign, rumors and threats fueled an environment brimming with distrust, suspicion and anxiety. The South African government and DTA supporters repeatedly spread rumors of PLAN members massing just over the Angolan border in preparation for an invasion and of SWAPO contingency plans underway for resuming the war if it lost the election.

South Africa made claims, which were unsubstantiated, of impending PLAN invasions several times during the transition. Just days before the election, for example, South African foreign minister Pik Botha announced the interception of UNTAG communications that warned of up to 600 PLAN fighters massing along Namibia's northern border preparing to attack. The intercepted messages turned out to be fraudulent and the Foreign Minister subsequently apologized, but the incident increased tensions and demonstrated the danger rumors posed when cast into such a volatile environment.

Many of the rumors were preposterous. Each side's partisans floated rumors about the misleading campaign tactics of the other. Often these included accusations about how to mark the ballot; i.e., large numbers of people were being taught to draw their cross on the ballot next to the party they wanted to vote *against* or were being told to make a large "X" across the entire ballot. One DTA official claimed that the ink used to demonstrate that someone had voted, which was supposed to last for at least the duration of the balloting period, might disappear within two days, thus opening the door to multiple voting.

The highly partisan nature of the newspapers and broadcast media also contributed to the spread of rumors. The overall result was a severe information problem to which UNTAG was incapable of responding.

Responses to the Problem of Intimidation

Code of Conduct

Responding to a proposal by the SR, the nine then-certifed parties prepared and signed a code of conduct on September 12 in Windhoek. (Appendix XV.) The code declared that "[a]n essential part of free and fair elections is freedom of political campaigning." It stated the right of everyone to express political views "without threat or fear" and recognized the responsibility of everyone "to accept every other person's freedom to campaign." The code condemned intimidation and the possession of weapons. It committed the parties, *inter alia*, to give advance notice of rallies to CIVPOL and SWAPOL; to attempt to avoid confrontations and disruptions of rallies; to refrain from inflammatory speeches or written materials; to use good offices to ensure reasonable access of all parties to potential voters on farms, state-owned properties, and the like; to attend regular meetings under UN auspices; and to honor the results of the election if the SR certified it as free and fair.

Signing the code of conduct marked a very significant and positive development in the campaign. The code, and the regular meetings among party leaders, created an important self-policing mechanism and encouraged the parties to exercise self-restraint.

Commission on Intimidation

In May, responding to the pervasive problem of intimidation, the AG formed the Commission for the Prevention and Combating of Intimidation and Election Malpractices, commonly referred to as the O'Linn Commission after its chairman, Judge Bryan O'Linn, a long-time civil rights activist and the founder of NPP 435. The commission comprised four members, a panel of attorneys and two investigators. However, it was O'Linn's role as chairman that provided the commission with credibility among Namibia's different ethnic groups and internationally.

The commission was empowered to submit written questions to witnesses and persons accused of intimidation, to subpoena witnesses and to hold public hearings. Although the commission did not possess the power to convict and sentence, it attempted to expose and deter intimidation by publicizing findings of fact. It also had the power to enjoin practices that amounted to intimidation, and it could refer criminal offenses to the attorney general for prosecution. Finally, the commission could recommend to the Administrator-General that he amend certain laws or fire certain officials.

The O'Linn Commission's strength stemmed from its ability to focus attention on the problem of intimidation. By raising public consciousness, the commission sought to deter additional intimidation, particularly among members of the police and other security forces. For example, the commission found political intimidation against two police officers who assaulted a man near Katima Mulilo, forced him to accept a UDF membership card and ordered him to solicit additional members for the party. In another incident involving the same officers, however, the commission ruled that there was insufficient evidence to conclude that the officers intended to intimidate a SWAPO organizer. The commission also investigated violence at a DTA rally in Katutura, finding sufficient evidence of criminal offenses directed against certain DTA organizers to refer the case to the attorney general for prosecution.

According to the chairman of the commission, due to juridical problems, UNTAG did not cooperate with the commission and would not allow its personnel to appear as witnesses. UNTAG referred only one case to the commission for investigation.

By the time the commission terminated operations on November 17, it had made formal findings in 128 of the 215 formal complaints it had received.

The commission's work received mixed reviews. Several political party leaders appreciated the commission's efforts in focussing attention on the intimidation problem and demonstrating that even police could be reprimanded by a government body. Others were less congratulatory. As one DTA leader commented: "The O'Linn Commission amounted to the biggest waste of time -- it was based on an assumption that complete peace was possible after years of fighting."

Campaign Rallies

Party rallies played an important part of the campaign. DTA rallies were characterized by the presence of continuous musical entertainment and food. SWAPO rallies, by contrast, were often more solemn events, featuring leaders who had recently returned from exile. Both parties transported people to rallies in open cattle trucks. Hats, shirts and skirts in party colors were very much in evidence at all political rallies.

Due to the recurring threat of violence, the Provision for the Protection of the Public Peace and Order at Public Gatherings proclamation (Proclamation AG 23) was adopted in August; it required notifying the police three days prior to assembling any political rally or other gathering of 20 or more people. (A similar law had been repealed as discriminatory by Proclamation AG 14.) Under AG 23, failure to give notice constituted an illegal gathering and subjected it to dispersal by the police. Ostensibly this requirement was intended to give the police and their UNTAG counterparts the opportunity to prepare for rallies, and thus to prevent violence, but observers supported SWAPO's claim of selective enforcement. In August, for example, it was reported that police dispersed a 3,000-person SWAPO rally in Arandis because organizers had mistakenly filed their intention to assemble with the local magistrate rather than with the police. SWAPO and the Legal Assistance Center, a local human rights law firm, called for the law's repeal, although UNTAG supported the concept of pre-rally notification.

Overall, though, rallies were essentially violence free. Only in a few cases, during the agitated atmosphere following the end of a rally, did rally participants clash with partisans of other parties.

The Campaign

Campaign Issues

Two parties, SWAPO and DTA, dominated the Namibian political campaign. For the most part, the campaign did not focus on policy issues. Rather SWAPO emphasized that the elections provided the opportunity for self-determination, decolonization and independence from South Africa, while the other nine participating parties directed criticisms at SWAPO.

As discussed above, the illegal detention and mistreatment of political prisoners by SWAPO became one of the most prominent issues in the campaign. Virtually all non-SWAPO political leaders criticized SWAPO's treatment of its prisoners and played up allegations of continuing detentions. They tried to link these allegations to the human rights policy of a future SWAPO government. SWAPO failed to respond effectively to the charges and allowed the issue to linger for months. The issue became an albatross for the party, undercutting its claim for the high moral ground and probably reducing its margin of victory.

SWAPO's opponents also questioned SWAPO's commitment to a multi-party system, particularly when SWAPO objected to incorporating the 1982 constitutional principles into the Constituent Assembly law. Many of SWAPO's opponents issued dire warnings about SWAPO's alleged intention to impose or create a single-party, authoritarian state.

Ethnicity seemed to be a major issue, albeit a generally tacit one. Many political leaders accused SWAPO of being solely the party of the Ovambo majority and of seeking to impose Ovambo domination upon the country's other ethnic groups. Many expressed concern about SWAPO's tolerance of other ethnic groups -- especially whites. Such arguments were in part a legacy of apartheid, introduced to Namibia by South African whites. In any event, SWAPO's list of candidates for the Constituent Assembly suggested the charges were largely unfounded. More than half of SWAPO's top 50 candidates were not Ovambo. Vice President Hendrik Witbooi, a Nama traditional leader, and four whites were slated in top positions on the party's list.

Many of those campaigning against SWAPO also tried to make a personal issue of Sam Nujoma. *Ad hominem* attacks against Nujoma were common, and SWAPO opponents sarcastically addressed campaign posters and slogans to "Sam." However, SWAPO supporters viewed Nujoma's persona as an asset, and thus his likeness was visible everywhere, from T-shirts and dresses to posters.

The DTA and other parties of the center and right warned that SWAPO would pursue a socialist economy -- nationalizing industries and expropriating private agricultural property. They argued that a SWAPO government would destroy the country's physical infrastructure. SWAPO maintained that it was committed to a "mixed economy." Although economic policy was certainly an important and substantive campaign issue, the economic debate -- like much of the campaign rhetoric -- seemed to generate more heat than light.

Finally, the conduct of the campaign became an issue. Problems of intimidation and campaign violence, and related allegations of cheating and unfairness, were sources of substantial campaign debate. SWAPO complained of large numbers of white South Africans entering the country to register to vote; they also alleged that the DTA was arranging to transport Angolans who supported UNITA across the northern border to vote. DTA alleged that Angolans of the Ovambo group and Zambians were planning to enter Namibia to vote illegally for SWAPO. SWAPO and DTA officials each accused one another's supporters of assault and intimidation. SWAPO partisans complained of South African interference and destabilization. DTA and other party leaders complained about the UN's alleged lack of impartiality.

Symbols

Each party's symbol appeared next to its name on the ballot. Given the high rate of illiteracy, party symbols assumed a major role in communicating identity, and each party made a concerted effort to publicize its symbol. No outside observer could fail to learn, for example, that DTA's symbol depicted two fingers raised in the shape of a "V" or that the SWAPO symbol used an arm and fist extended straight up into the air. Nine parties used symbols that included a hand, four of which made the hand into a fist.

SWAPO, in particular, had to accentuate its symbol because the SWAPO-Democrats, a separate political party, not only used a confusingly similar name, but also adopted the torch symbol previously used by SWAPO for more than 20 years. In some mock elections, significant numbers of presumably confused voters reportedly cast their ballots by mistake for the SWAPO-D torch instead of the SWAPO fist. In the end, however, there was apparently no such confusion, since SWAPO-D garnered only about 3,000 votes, not enough to win a single seat.

Improvement in Atmosphere before Election

Adherence to the code of conduct and other efforts by political leaders and UNTAG contributed to a substantial lessening of intimidation during the last weeks of the campaign. The contrast between the political atmosphere in May and that in November was astounding; while in May people appeared intimidated, by the election period their inhibitions were replaced with expressions of political loyalties. Party T-shirts were ubiquitous; clothes and umbrellas in party colors were also visible everywhere. Houses, businesses and trees throughout the country were adorned with party flags and political posters were prominently displayed. Leaflets, some of questionable taste, were also widespread.

Chapter 7
MEDIA AND INFORMATION

Broadcast Media

The broadcast media, particularly radio, played an extremely important role in both the election campaign and the UNTAG effort. Since an estimated 60 percent of Namibians are illiterate, radio broadcasts were critical to the dissemination of voter education information, political messages and news. Paid political advertising, however, was prohibited.

SWABC.

The South West Africa Broadcasting Corporation (SWABC), a parastatal company established in 1979, controls the broadcast media. Since SWABC's inception, the SWA government has subsidized the corporation at a reported rate of R25 million (about $10 million) per year. SWABC broadcasts radio programs in 13 languages on eight FM channels, which reach most of the population. The single television station broadcasts primarily in Afrikaans only during the evening hours each day.

The Administrator-General officially appointed the SWABC board of directors and controlled the company's budget. Responding to criticism of SWABC election coverage, several members of the governing board resigned during the campaign, and the board declared itself "in recess until further notice" on October 27, just 10 days before the start of the election. The AG neither appointed new board members nor established an editorial committee to provide policy guidance. Election coverage was left in the hands of the station managers.

Broadcast Access and News Coverage

In June, SWABC invited representatives of 14 political parties to consult on election coverage and organized a standing consultative committee. The television station subsequently established a schedule for the broadcast of each registered party's campaign message and provided five minutes of air time to two parties each night during the last six weeks before the elections.

There was similar "equal" treatment in the news coverage of political rallies, press conferences and media releases. By self-imposed agreement, each party was allocated coverage on a rotating alphabetical basis.

Despite this ostensibly fair system for covering political events, a Namibian Peace Plan 435 study, which monitored radio and television broadcasts over a four month period, concluded that SWABC news coverage of the electoral process was "extremely selective and deliberately one-sided in its choice of information broadcast." The broadcasting company's "selective choice of content in editing and compiling of news bulletins" was, according to the study, "aimed at supporting the current status quo," and its coverage of SWAPO was overwhelmingly negative. As examples, the study noted: the repeated references to April 1 and unsubstantiated reports of additional SWAPO incursions; the failure to mention hostile actions by members of Koevoet; economic reporting that alluded to a free market system as a prerequisite for future foreign aid; and "maximum coverage" of allegations about SWAPO detentions even when no significant developments could be detailed. The report also highlighted the discriminatory placement of news stories in relation to their importance. SWABC's news report about the massive SWAPO rally for Nujoma when he returned to the country was the third story in the broadcast -- the lead story featured Dirk Mudge of DTA claiming that his party would adhere to the code of conduct. In one period, out of 20 news items about SWAPO, the study judged that 16 were "negative"; only one contained live footage. In the same period, eight of 10 items featuring DTA were judged to be positive.

The placement of stories on the morning radio news following the previous night's announcement of the election results provided a particularly bizarre example of SWABC's orientation. The lead story was a statement by the Administrator-General, and it was followed by the comments of the South Africa's president. The election results and the story of SWAPO's victory were the third story reported.

The one-sided political propaganda aired by SWABC distorted the media coverage of the election. SWABC proved to be the one institution on which UNTAG failed to have an impact.

Voter Education

SWABC provided air time for voter education messages. In May, SWABC offered UNTAG five minutes of radio time daily and 10 minutes on a weekly TV slot. UNTAG was unprepared to produce the public information and communications program that the situation demanded, and did not begin to use its broadcast time until late June. SWABC complained that UNTAG used its air time for public relations instead of voter education. In their defense, UNTAG officials claimed that programming had been hampered by the delayed arrival of members of the relevant UN communications team; they had been denied visas by the South African government. More significantly, there were differences of opinion within the UN about the content of the UNTAG message. Some believed that they could produce educational messages about the UN and Resolution 435, while others wanted to use the programs to build confidence in the election process.

UNTAG eventually implemented a program to encourage voter participation, to help voters cast their ballots in an informed manner and to assure the population that balloting would take place in secret. The UNTAG information programs utilized newspapers, advertising, posters and leaflets. The regional and district UNTAG officials displayed instructional videos and films, addressed community meetings, and engaged in other public education activities.

The thrust of UNTAG's voter education efforts was to reassure people about the secrecy of their ballots, and the Administrator-General's education campaign struck a similar theme. The AG's office launched a major advertising campaign in July which cost R1.4 million (about $600,000). The campaign used broadcast media, brochures, newspaper advertisements and billboards to convey in numerous languages throughout the country the messages "vote without fear" and "your vote is your secret." The AG's use of a multi-colored rainbow logo suggested unity to some observers and reinforced South Africa's policy of emphasizing separate ethnic groups to others.

Print Media

In contrast to the state monopoly over the broadcast media, the press in Namibia is vigorous and vociferous. With the exception of the trilingual *Namibian Times* published in Walvis Bay, all newspapers are published in Windhoek. The two most widely-circulated dailies are *Die Republikein*, an Afrikaans newspaper generally supportive of the AG and the DTA, and *The Namibian*, an English-language paper generally viewed as aligned with SWAPO. Both of these papers have a daily circulation of approximately 13,000. Other dailies include the long-established *Windhoek Advertiser*, a right-wing paper traditionally supportive of the National Party; *Algemeine Zeitung*, a German newspaper that is also pro-National Party; and *Die Suidwester*, another Afrikaans paper. There are two weekly papers: the *Windhoek Observer*, an English-language weekly, and *The Namibian Northern*, a German left-wing paper. These newspapers are all highly partisan.

While the government retained the legal authority to censor, or even shut down, any paper of which it disapproved, it did not threaten to use this power during the campaign. As previously noted, however, the editor of *The Namibian* received several death threats during the campaign.

Chapter 8
ELECTION

Balloting

More than 97 percent of the 701,483 registered Namibian voters cast ballots during the election period. They voted at 408 polling stations, 265 of which were in fixed locations for the entire five-day period and 143 of which were mobile units that stopped in several locations during the voting period. In response to the scheduling problems mobile teams encountered during the registration period, authorities altered their original plans to emphasize mobile units by increasing the number of fixed sites and reducing the number of traveling units. In Ovamboland, for example, there were 124 fixed locations and 13 mobile teams.

Polling sites were located in schools, community halls and other public buildings, while mobile units often established balloting positions outdoors. At each polling site, there were placed tables around which polling officials and their UNTAG counterparts sat. Also at each site were ballot boxes for completed ballots and registration cards, one to four ballot booths, an ultraviolet light machine to check for the dye affixed to a voter's hand once he or she had voted, a pad of consecutively-numbered ballot papers, and envelopes for tendered ballots.

Civil servants served as AG electoral officials. Typically, five AG officials were on hand; they wore white shirts with the AG's rainbow logo on the sleeve and above the pocket. They were assisted by four UNTAG officials who wore blue UNTAG armbands with the UN seal. The entrance and exit of each polling site were guarded by SWAPOL and CIVPOL police. Political party agents sat in the room, but were situated relatively removed from the tables. They did not wear anything to indicate party affiliation.

58

The ballot itself was a white sheet of paper, approximately 8 1/2" by 11", torn from a numbered pad. It included the names and symbols of each of the 10 parties printed in black ink. (Appendix XVI.)

Election Procedures

Notwithstanding the mid-course changes in the election procedures, the final balloting system was highly cumbersome. In an effort to prevent fraud, it involved extensive and redundant identity checks.

First, a voter had to produce both a registration card and an identification card. In addition, a polling officer was allowed to ask the voter his/her name and address, whether the signature or thumbprint on the registration card was his/hers, where he/she had registered, and whether he/she had already voted. To determine if there were any questions regarding the person's registration, an election official would then check the voter's name against three lists: a list of objections to registration, a list of cancelled registration cards, and a list of persons who registered more than once.

Once past this test, the voter would sign his/her name or put his/her thumbprint on the registration card. Next, the voter put his/her hand under an ultraviolet light to demonstrate the absence of the ink that would be present if he/she had voted previously. Finally, to mark the voter so that he/she could not vote again, he/she would dip his/her fingers in a transparent liquid dye that would be visible for a week under ultraviolet light.

Only after all of these checks had been satisfied would an election officer place an official stamp on a blank ballot and give it to the voter. The officer would explain how to mark the ballot, and the voter would proceed to the voting booth. After marking his/her choice, the voter would refold the ballot in a manner to ensure secrecy, show the official stamp to another election official, and deposit the ballot in the ballot box.

A voter who lacked an identity document, but who had a registration card, was required to have another registered voter, who had not yet voted, sign an affidavit attesting to the first voter's identity. A voter so identified was eligible to cast an ordinary ballot, however, as opposed to a tendered one.

Tendered Ballots

Certain voters were required to cast "tendered ballots," which were verified and centrally counted in Windhoek. These were: 1) individuals voting somewhere other than the district in which they were registered;

2) persons who had lost their registration cards; 3) persons who appeared to have registered more than once; and 4) persons whose identity was challenged or questioned, either by officials or by party polling agents. A voter without registration card could vote after making a declaration attesting to the fact that he/she was registered.

The tendered ballot procedure required a voter to place his/her ballot in a special envelope. After marking his/her ballot and enclosing it in the envelope, the voter would give the envelope to the presiding officer. The presiding officer would put the first envelope with the registration card or declaration of registration in a second envelope. The fficer would place that envelope in a special box for tendered ballots.

Balloting Process in Operation

In view of the fears expressed during the campaign, the balloting process must, in the final analysis, be judged a major success. Significantly, there were no credible allegations of fraud in the balloting and counting processes. There were, however, several notable administrative problems.

Delays in sorting out and announcing details of the electoral system plagued the process. The AG's office did not complete the announcement of polling sites until the first day of voting. Indeed, until the last minute, UNTAG and the AG were negotiating over the need for additional polling stations in Ovamboland.

During the first two days of polling, exceedingly long lines were reported throughout the territory. On the first day, some polling stations, reported hundreds of voters in line hours before the polls were to open at 7 a.m. It was the beginning of summer in Namibia, and the temperature registered over 100 degrees Fahrenheit by mid-morning in some places. While the crowds were generally well-behaved and orderly, at some locations people reportedly became impatient with the slow pace. At several stations the crush of crowds left some people injured, although the reports of a baby being crushed to death in Oshikuku proved false. By contrast, in Keetmanshoop, the community set up a makeshift cafeteria and provided free breakfast and lunch for those people waiting to vote; as people arrived they were given a reservation number and could relax and avail themselves of food and drink until they were called to rejoin the line, in groups of 50. Overall, 33 percent of the population voted on the first day of balloting.

By Wednesday, the second day of voting, a combination of smaller crowds, a day's worth of experience for election officials, and an increased police presence resolved most of the crowd control problems. At one location in Ovamboland, for example, officials unrolled barbed wire to mark the place for the queue and to prevent waiting voters from disorderly massing outside the polling station. At several stations, officials improvised an express lane by splitting voters into two lines -- those who possessed proper identification and those who did not; this prevented the cumbersome process of identifying voters by affidavit from slowing the entire line. Thirty-two percent of the registered population voted on Wednesday. By Thursday, the amount of voters dramatically decreased, with 19 percent of the registered population voting. The numbers tapered off to fewer still by Friday and Saturday, the final two days.

The most significant balloting problem occurred in Ovambo, where, at a number of locations, the supply of blank ballot papers was insufficient. Some polling stations actually had to close for varying periods of time due to a lack of ballots. People who had waited for many hours were forced to leave polling stations before they had a chance to vote. On the third day of the voting period, 13 polling stations were closed for lack of materials, and on the following day, 17 closed for at least part of the day. All stations were not open again simultaneously until Saturday, the final day of polling. Some observer groups, already suspicious of official manipulation, believed that their fears had been realized with the closings and delays. However, even these groups ultimately acknowledged that the closures had not deprived more than a very few prospective voters their right to cast a ballot.

Officials explained that the ballot supply problem stemmed from unintentionally miscalculating voting patterns based on the registration experience. That is, substantial numbers of people voted in places other than where they registered. Although officials supplied enough blank ballots in the aggregate to Ovambo, for instance, their allocation did not correspond to voting patterns. In any event, with substantial logistical assistance from UNTAG, election officials made a reasonable effort to transfer excess ballots from some locations to other polling stations where they were in short supply. In addition, church groups, political parties, businessmen and local community leaders worked together to mitigate the ballot-shortage difficulties by organizing transportation for potential voters to locations with adequate supplies. The quick response of the community and the success of the transportation effort probably prevented the problem from disenfranchising large numbers of people, thus defusing possible violent repercussions.

The creation of special polling stations for the convenience of individuals coming to Namibia from South Africa posed another problem. Officials established polling stations on the South African border at Ariamsvlei and Noordoewer, where people were transported by bus convoys from the Cape and Orange Free State provinces. At the Windhoek airport, polling officials allowed South African whites, who arrived on chartered flights, to wait in special lines separate from the local population voting at the same polling station. After stern objections from UNTAG and an outcry in the press, officials halted such preferential treatment.

Political disinformation activities were also in evidence during the voting period. On the first two days of balloting, aircraft dropped over populated areas political leaflets, purported to be from SWAPO. One leaflet included a message that claimed to be from Hage Geingob, SWAPO's election director, urging people to wait until Thursday or Friday to vote. Another "confidential" message alleged to be from Sam Nujoma told certain PLAN members (those from Sam Nujoma's native region) that they would receive favorable salary treatment as compared to other PLAN members. At UNTAG's request, the AG's office ran radio spots to counter the disinformation, but they were probably unnecessary because few people seemed to be fooled. The disinformation effort was clumsy at best, and by Thursday the local DTA leader in Ovambo was trying desperately to distance himself from the pamphlets.

Various other problems arose at the balloting locations. Polling officials often placed party polling agents too far from the voter verification process for the agents to serve much of a purpose. Interpreters were often in short supply, and in some locations there was an occasional voter who spoke a language for which none was available. The interpreter in Grootfontein, for instance, could not communicate with one elderly Damara woman, and she apparently never learned how to mark her ballot. Vociferous partisans in party colors sometimes stepped inside the 500-meter zone that was to be free of party activity, and DTA supporters in Ovamboland placed political posters on the walls inside polling stations during the first days of balloting. Election officials in some locations incorrectly required tendered ballots of individuals identified by affidavit. There were also various instances where officials entered the polling booths apparently to help voters cast ballots, but in direct violation of the election law; in one case, officials reportedly allowed a tribal headman to accompany voters into the polling booth. There were also unconfirmed reports of mobile units leaving polling locations before everyone waiting in line could vote. Some problems were undoubtedly inevitable, given the population's widespread illiteracy and inexperience with elections, not to mention the delayed creation of the electoral system and the last-minute announcement of polling sites. Yet, despite the distrust with which the AG's government was viewed by large segments of the Namibian population and the international community, even skeptical observers did not witness any calculated effort to disenfranchise citizens.

Transportation of Ballots to Counting Centers

Paralleling the care taken with the balloting procedures, polling officers supervised by UNTAG election officials followed elaborate procedures to secure the ballot boxes and prevent tampering. At the conclusion of each day, ballot boxes were sealed with wire and affixed with AG and UNTAG seals. SWAPOL and CIVPOL officers guarded the boxes. At the end of the five-day balloting period, election officials guarded by SWAPOL and CIVPOL, transported the boxes of ballots and other election materials to the district centers. In remote areas, polling teams waited until they were joined by other teams to form convoys. Ballot boxes arrived at the district counting centers throughout the day on Sunday, November 12.

During this period, several armed men threatened the security of the Ovambo district counting center at Ongwediva. UNTAG and SWAPOL officials took extensive precautions to protect the building, both before and during the count. They surrounded the building with barbed wire and parked casspirs in front of the entrances. Heavily armed SWA police personnel, accompanied by CIVPOL officers, prominently guarded the facility.

Counting, Verification and Tabulation

Counting of ordinary (non-tendered) ballots took place on November 13 and 14 in 23 district counting centers located throughout the country. Tendered ballots were transported to Windhoek after each day's balloting to begin the process of verification. There were 92,856 tendered ballots, approximately 13.6 percent of the total number cast. In addition, a random sample of about 20 percent of the registration cards associated with ordinary ballots was also sent to Windhoek for verification against the Central Registry. A total of 680,688 votes were cast. Officials rejected 9,858 ballots, or about 1.4 percent of the total, as invalid, either because they were considered spoiled (i.e., the intention of the voter could not be definitely determined) or they were rejected as illegitimate (i.e., they were not cast by eligible voters). Thus, 670,830 ballots were certified as valid. The counting process proceeded in an efficient manner. In most of the 23 districts, the count was completed on Monday, November 13. Only in the larger districts of Ovambo and Kavango did the count continue into the night.

In Ovambo, the largest district, a sizable team of government election officials and their UNTAG counterparts assembled before 7 a.m. in a large assembly hall at the Ongwediva community school. After receiving instructions from the chief officer, they began the laborious process of unfolding, sorting and counting the paper ballots. Initially they sorted the ballots into 10 boxes, one for each of the parties. Eventually, though, to accommodate the overwhelming majority of the ballots marked for SWAPO, the counters abandoned the boxes and sorted and bundled SWAPO ballots in batches of 20. Despite extreme heat, government and UNTAG officials worked side-by-side throughout the day and into the night with virtually no rest breaks.

At one point after nightfall, the electricity at Ongwediva suddenly failed, and the entire room was plunged into darkness. Within moments, various people produced flashlights, a foreign camera crew turned on its camera lights, and officials went outside, turned on vehicle headlights, and aimed them into the school windows. Counting resumed as if nothing had happened. (Officials later ruled out sabotage; sudden electricity failures are not unheard of in Africa.) Thirty minutes later the lights were restored, and the count continued until it was completed after midnight. Ovamboland was the last district to report its results, which it did on Tuesday morning.

Certification of Election as Free and Fair

Under the Settlement Plan, the Special Representative was responsible for supervising and certifying the fairness of all phases of the electoral process. On Saturday, November 11, after the close of polls throughout the territory, Ahtisaari announced that he was satisfied that "the voting process has been free and fair" and that counting should begin. On Tuesday, November 14, he formally certified that "the electoral process in Namibia has at each stage been free and fair, and that it has been conducted to my satisfaction."

Election Results

Seven parties won seats in the 72-member Constituent Assembly. SWAPO received almost 385,000 votes or about 57.3 percent of the total, which entitled it to 41 seats. DTA was second, winning 21 seats, having garnered almost 192,000 votes or 28.6 percent. The United Democratic Front of Namibia (UDF) won four seats with about 38,000 votes (5.6 percent), the Action Christian National (ACN) gained three seats with just under 24,000 votes (3.5 percent), the National Patriotic Front of Namibia (NPF) and the Federal Convention of Namibia (FCN) won one seat each with about 10,000 votes (1.6 percent), and the Namibian National Front (NNF) captured one seat with just over 5,000 votes (0.8 percent).

More than one-third of the total votes cast were in the Ovambo district, where SWAPO won 92 percent of the ballots (225,000 of 245,000). In the Windhoek district, the second largest with 96,000 votes, SWAPO and DTA obtained 45.9 percent and 36 percent, respectively. In Kavango, the third largest district with almost 60,000 votes, SWAPO received 51.7 percent and the DTA received 41.7 percent.

The UDF's strongest showing was in Damaraland, where it won almost 8,000 of the 15,000 votes (52 percent). DTA carried Herroland with almost two-thirds of the 15,000 votes to SWAPO's 15 percent. The ACN's strongest showing was in Karasburg on the South African border, where the party received just under 5,000 votes (25.7 percent); DTA obtained 53.9 percent in the same district. (Appendix XVII.)

Chapter 9

THE UNITED NATIONS TRANSITION ASSISTANCE GROUP

Unique UN Role in Namibia

The UNTAG operation in Namibia marks a dramatic development in UN peacekeeping and decolonization efforts. To assist in the transition to independence, UNTAG involved international military personnel and civilian police monitors and election supervisors. Given the success of the operation, UNTAG suggests a new dimension for future UN roles in international conflict resolution.

The term "peacekeeping" is now applied to those operations where the UN introduces multinational military forces under international command into hostile situations to control or resolve conflicts. Secretary-General Perez de Cuellar has described United Nations peacekeeping as "keeping belligerents at arm's length so that negotiations for a more permanent peace can go forward." The Security Council will authorize peacekeeping operations only with the consent of the countries involved, and Security Council approval of any given operation necessarily implies broad international support.

The UN Charter guarantees the right of dependent people to self-determination, and the Declaration on the Granting of Independence to Colonial Countries and Peoples sanctions the extension of this right beyond Trust Territories to all non-self-governing peoples covered by Chapter XI of the Charter. The General Assembly's Fourth Committee has jurisdiction over decolonization. It oversees a list of 19 non-self-governing territories that until independence included Namibia. Prior to the Namibia operation, UN representatives had been involved in approximately 30 elections, plebiscites and referendums in the decolonization context, but usually with a limited mandate and with a relatively small on-site team.

The UNTAG operation in Namibia, however, was neither a traditional peacekeeping effort nor a mere election-monitoring operation. Though it borrowed certain features from both kinds of UN operations, UNTAG was unique. It combined a military role, organized along the lines of a peacekeeping effort, with an extensive role in an election process designed to resolve a long-standing conflict. It required the active involvement of a large number of UN member states; the very size and scope of the civilian operation was unprecedented, and the military force was the largest deployed by the UN since it sent 19,000 troops to the Belgian Congo, now Zaire, in 1960. The operation had an extremely long gestation period, over a decade between inception and implementation. Finally, unlike oversight undertaken in other decolonization efforts, the Security Council, rather than the General Assembly, controlled the operation in Namibia.

Organization and Structure of UNTAG

General Administration

Both the civilian and military components of UNTAG operated under the authority of the Special Representative. UNTAG's civilian force structure included the Office of the Special Representative, the Deputy Special Representative, the Election Unit, the Police Adviser and the Chief Administrative Officer.

The Secretary-General appointed Martti Ahtisaari as Special Representative in 1978 and Prem Chand as military commander in 1980. Ahtisaari designated Cedric Thornberry as Director of the Special Representative's office in 1978. The Secretary-General created the office of Deputy Special Representative in June 1989 and appointed Joseph Legwaila to that post.

A total of about 8,000 individuals from 110 countries served in Namibia during the course of the UNTAG operation. More than 1,000 individuals from the United Nations Secretariat participated as part of the civilian UNTAG effort, and member countries contributed a total of 1,500 civilian police officers, more than 1,500 election supervisors, and more than 4,500 military personnel.

UNTAG personnel arrived in Namibia in three phases. The first group of civilian and military personnel arrived in Namibia around April 1, the beginning of the transition period. A second phase group arrived in the summer and assisted in the registration process. The final group of election supervisors from member countries and from the Secretariat arrived in the weeks before the election.

Regional and District Offices

UNTAG's headquarters were located in Windhoek, and it established 42 political offices in 10 regions throughout the territory, all of which were operational by June. Two professionals generally staffed each office.

Upon their arrival in the field, UNTAG officials contacted political leaders, clergy members and tribal headmen. They worked with local party and other leaders to provide information on the transition process, to receive feedback from the local population, and to assist as much as possible in the reconciliation process by bringing all sides together.

The field offices were the backbone of the UNTAG operations; the men and women in these posts succeeded in instilling confidence in the local population regarding the transition process. The makeshift offices with the blue flags flying in remote areas of Namibia were quite distant geographically and culturally from New York and Geneva. Though officers filed daily reports with UNTAG headquarters in Windhoek, of necessity they relied on personal intuition and practical experience in the field for guidance in daily decision making.

UNTAG Civilian Police

The Settlement Plan provided that CIVPOL monitor the activities of the South West African Police, which retained primary responsibility for maintaining law and order during the transition period. The original Plan called for 360 UNTAG police monitors, but the Secretary-General's report in January 1989 increased the number to 500. Armed with information from the field, Ahtisaari twice requested the deployment of additional police monitors, and upon the recommendation of the Secretary-General, the Security Council approved an additional 500 police officers in May and 500 more in September.

As of November 9, there were 1,498 police officers deployed throughout the territory. The largest number, more than 600, were in Ovamboland, divided between Ondangwa and Oshakati. There were 260 assigned to the Windhoek district, almost 200 each at Otjiwarongo and Rundu, about 100 each at Keetmanshoop and Gobabis, and approximately 50 at UNTAG headquarters. These monitors were drawn from 25 countries, with the largest numbers (more than 100 each) from Nigeria, Pakistan, Ghana, Fiji and Canada. According to UNTAG, approximately 900 complaints were presented to CIVPOL regarding alleged abuses by SWAPOL personnel. These complaints were forwarded to the AG. Neither the Settlement Plan nor the terms of reference provided CIVPOL with authority to initiate investigations, question witnesses or make arrests.

Election Unit

The Electoral Division of UNTAG, with the assistance of the Director of Legal Affairs (Szasz), was responsible for helping to develop an effective electoral system. Notwithstanding ambiguities in the Settlement Plan about the extent of UNTAG's role in developing electoral legislation, senior UNTAG election officials exercised considerable influence over the election process, in developing both the law and the procedures, and in providing important administrative help.

Election Supervisors

UNTAG recruited about 1,700 electoral supervisors from 26 countries. Denmark, Kenya, Nigeria, Pakistan, Thailand and the United Kingdom each contributed 40 or more officials; more than 30 each were nationals of Canada, Finland, France, West Germany, Ghana, Norway, Poland, Sweden, Switzerland, and Trinidad and Tobago.

The election supervisors were theoretically selected on the basis of their experience, fluency in English, tempermental suitability to live in harsh conditions, and ability to drive transport vehicles. The contributing governments recruited the supervisors and paid their salaries. UNTAG maintained operational control and paid costs associated with the supervisor's service, such as transportation, food and lodging.

The electoral supervisors joined UNTAG during the last weeks before the election. After attending a four-day training session, they were assigned to teams and dispersed throughout the country. During the balloting period, these officials monitored every detail of the balloting process. In most cases, a spirit of cooperation and even camaraderie between the government civil servants and UNTAG election officials became the norm, rather than the exception.

Military Force.

Three major battalions, one each from Kenya, Malaysia and Finland, constituted the bulk of the military force. The military component also included signals, medical, military police, air, logistics and military observer units. The Settlement Plan assigned several functions to the UNTAG military force. First, it was responsible for monitoring the cessation of hostilities, the restriction to base of South African and SWAPO armed forces and the phased withdrawal of most South African troops. Second, the military was charged with responsibility for surveillance and preventing infiltration of the borders. Third, the Plan called on the military to monitor the demobilization of the citizen forces, commandos and ethnic forces. The military could also assist the police, if called upon to do so. In fact, the military guarded UNTAG offices throughout the territory.

The military provided substantial logistical support to the field operations and electoral supervisors. The British signals unit established an excellent communication system throughout Namibia, a system that was vital to the success of the election operation. Australian engineers also modified and built facilities and provided similar support as needed, and an Italian helicopter unit transported mobile election teams and ballot boxes. In addition, they provided humanitarian assistance, such as water delivery and clearance of mines, in many parts of the country.

As discussed previously, the Security Council debated changes to the Settlement Plan between December 1988 and April 1989. Most important, at the insistence of the permanent members, the Council limited the size of the UNTAG military contingent. The 1978 plan fixed the size of the military contingent at 7,500, although even then it was anticipated that a smaller number would be deployed. In early 1989, the Security Council authorized a military force of 4,650, comprising three enlarged infantry battalions, 300 military observers, about 1,700 logistics troops and a headquarters staff of about 100. As of October 12, 4,327 UNTAG military personnel from 21 countries were located in the territory.

The battle concerning the size of the military component consumed a great deal of time and left UNTAG without significant forces deployed during the April conflict. UNTAG officials knew, as the original Settlement Plan provided, that they needed at least six weeks to deploy the operation, especially thc military force -- sufficient time to move personnel and equipment and to acquire supplies -- and thus the debate over force size delayed most of the deployment until after April 1.

Even if the full force of 7,500 troops had been deployed, however, it is arguable whether UNTAG could have prevented the fighting of April 1. In fact, during the negotiation of the Settlement Plan, SWAPO suggested that a force size as high as 30,000 would have been necessary. After April, the military played a relatively limited role. UNTAG military forces continued to monitor 1,700 troops remaining at bases in Grootfontein and Oshivelo, as well as to guard warehouses of weapons.

Planning for Deployment

Following a survey mission to Namibia in 1978, the Special Representative prepared a draft plan for UNTAG and began to recruit senior professional staff. Over the next decade, the SR and several other senior UNTAG officials periodically reviewed, revised and initiated arrangements to implement the plan, only to be stymied in each case by events beyond their control. In late 1988, when implementation of the Resolution 435 plan began to seem likely, United Nations officials and members of the Security Council reviewed once more the deployment plan, determining what modifications would be necessary in view of the changed circumstances.

Recruitment

As implementation became a real possibility, UNTAG circulated announcements throughout the UN seeking recruits for the Namibia operation. By December, more than 1,000 people had expressed a desire to volunteer, while many others indicated at least a potential interest.

In light of this response, Ahtisaari conducted an open meeting for all interested parties. The meeting disseminated information about Namibia and UNTAG's mission, but was also meant to discourage less committed volunteers. The briefing was apparently successful in presenting a realistic portrayal of expectations, and while some applicants withdrew, some new ones volunteered.

Diversity in staffing the operation was an important consideration, and there was in fact substantial geographic diversity in the civilian component. Ahtisaari consciously sought to include personnel from the Soviet Union and Eastern Europe, despite Western biases regarding their involvement in a mission designed to ensure free and fair elections. Ahtisaari also emphasized the recruitment of women and Africans. Women comprised over 45 percent of UNTAG and served as directors in three of the 10 regional offices. By the first week of February 1989, senior UNTAG officials had selected the top staff of the Special Representative's office and nine of the 10 regional directors.

Training

At Ahtisaari's request, the UN's Training Service, with the help of the training chief of the United Nation High Commissioner for Refugees, organized week-long training sessions for professional staff from the New York, Geneva and Vienna offices. These sessions included mission-specific briefings on Namibia, and more general training and case studies on team-building and emergency preparation. The training personnel also administered a parallel program for general service personnel. They did not have the opportunity to provide similar training for the UNTAG civilian police, although they did brief senior police officials in several countries involved in the selection of police contingents. Training continued into March, even while the status of the mission was uncertain due to the dispute over the size of the military contingent.

The Training Service also briefed the second wave of UN personnel, who arrived in Namibia in July to participate in the registration process. The UNTAG Election Unit conducted some training in Namibia, but the Secretariat did not participate in training until the election supervisors arrived in the fall.

UNTAG officials in Namibia developed comprehensive training materials for election supervisors. These materials summarized the terms of the election law and the corresponding exchange of letters, provided background on the Resolution 435 process, and detailed the role of UNTAG supervisors in the election process. During the week before the elections, Secretariat training personnel and UNTAG election experts led four-day training sessions in Namibia for newly-arrived election supervisors. These sessions were held in four locations: Windhoek, Rundu, Ongwediva and Keetmanshoop. They covered the details of the balloting process under the election law and provided information about logistics and formation of teams.

The emphasis on preparation of personnel was well placed, and the training program was apparently quite successful. The in-country training for election supervisors, for example, seemed careful and thorough. Trainers detailed the polling procedures and led mock polling exercises, raising a variety of hypothetical voting problems. The officials being trained were also serious and professional, and many had evidently read with care the detailed briefing materials. In some cases, in fact, the trainees asked very specific questions or posed highly nuanced hypothetical questions that the UNTAG trainers could not readily answer. The training program would have been enhanced if additional follow-up training could have been conducted in Namibia for personnel who arrived very early in the process.

Financing

The scale of the UNTAG operation made it extraordinarily expensive. One UNTAG official said that the UN "had to pay for the international community's paranoia about South Africa." In January 1989, the Secretary-General projected the final cost of the UNTAG operation to be $416 million, and the General Assembly approved essentially that budget in March. In December 1989, though, the Secretary-General placed actual requirements for the UNTAG operation at about $367 million, $49 million under the budget.

In his December report to the General Assembly on UNTAG financing, the Secretary-General analyzed the state of UNTAG's budget, discussed the status of assessed and voluntary contributions and presented a plan for the disposition and liquidation of UNTAG assets after the end of the operation. Based on performance-to-date and certain modified assumptions, and with provision for the estimated costs of a six-month liquidation phase, the Secretary-General's report projected that UNTAG would realize a net savings of $42.8 million.

The Secretary-General attributed the savings to voluntary contributions, in-cash and in-kind; shorter-than-projected stays for military and other personnel; savings of $7 million on accommodations; and savings of $21 million on air operations. At the same time, certain budget line items had been exceeded, especially for costs associated with providing additional police monitors, election supervisors and handwriting and fingerprint experts during the election.

As in peacekeeping operations, costs for the Namibian operation fell into three categories: 1) UN administrative costs, such as salaries of participating Secretariat employees; 2) purchases of goods and services for the UNTAG operation; and 3) reimbursements to governments that contributed personnel. Governments paid the salaries of the election supervisors and military personnel they provided, while the UN paid travel, living and other costs associated with their service. The UN, however, is obligated to reimburse governments contributing military and police personnel at a fixed rate, and it is responsible for the use of military equipment according to a four-year amortization schedule.

Assessments

Costs of the UNTAG operation were assessed in accordance with treaty obligations. Budgeted costs of almost $410 million were apportioned among UN member states as follows: $240 million from the five permanent members, $155 million from other economically-developed countries, $11 million from less-developed nations and some $2 million from the 47 least-developed countries. As of November 30, 1989, the UN had received only $315 million. Assessments of almost $95 million remain outstanding.

A number of governments made voluntary contributions to UNTAG. Germany, Greece, Switzerland and the United States made in-kind contributions valued at $10 million, and Japan contributed $13 million in cash.

In general, treaty obligations for contributions to peacekeeping operations impose a heavy burden on the permanent members; the United States is responsible for more than 30 percent of peacekeeping operations. As of February 3, the U.S. owed approximately $152.7 million on the peacekeeping accounts and was an additional $365 million in arrears to the UN general budget.

When, as in the case of UNTAG, member states fail to pay their full assessments, the UN gives priority to the first two categories of expenses -- i.e., UN salaries and purchases of goods and services -- and thus cannot pay obligations owed to contributing governments. The UN is about 10 years behind on payments to governments for their contributions of personnel to peacekeeping operations.

Chapter 10
EVALUATION OF UNTAG

Scope of UNTAG Mandate

In assessing the UN's Namibia operation, it is important to recognize the scope and limitations of UNTAG's mandate under Resolution 435. The Settlement Plan authorized UNTAG to "supervise and control" the elections. The Plan did not define this phrase, but it provided that the Special Representative be "satisfied" with the process at each stage, and implicitly left the administration of the process to the South African authorities. The inherent ambiguities, of the UN's "supervision and control" mandate *vis-à-vis* the reality of South African administration substantially contributed to many of the UN's implementation difficulties.

UNTAG's task was multidimensional; it had political, electoral, police, military, logistical, and administrative responsibilities. UNTAG's fundamental responsibilities were to monitor the AG's government and to attempt to guarantee an atmosphere free of intimidation. This was a compromise between actual UN administration and no UN role at all.

The role played by Special Representative was thus an extraordinarily difficult one. On the one hand, he was obliged to ensure that the elections were conducted in a free and fair manner and that the parties respected the instructions and demands of the various Security Council resolutions, Secretary-General reports and other diplomatic papers. On the other hand, he was under pressure to advance the process to a conclusion, thus making less credible his ultimate leverage to halt the process if dissatisfied with the measures taken by the Administrator-General. Given these competing pressures, the SR's job required Ahtisaari to draw on all of his diplomatic skills.

The UN civilian police monitors also felt constrained by the limits of their "monitoring" role. After the implementation of the Settlement Plan began, widespread intimidation and election-related violence posed more of a threat to the transition process than the possibility of renewed armed conflict. In this regard, the Settlement Plan's emphasis on responding to a military threat was outdated. As it became clear that the civilian police would have to play a particularly critical role, Ahtisaari twice found it necessary to request substantial increases in the number of CIVPOL officers. Ultimately, 1,500 were deployed, triple the number in the field at the beginning of April and more than four times the 360 provided for in the original Settlement Plan.

The unreasonable expectations of many segments of the Namibian population and the international community and the suspicions of the major protagonists, further complicated UNTAG's task. The South Africans suspected that the UN desired a SWAPO victory in the elections. Many SWAPO members felt that UNTAG bent over backwards to demonstrate its impartiality, while other parties participating in the elections were convinced that the UN favored SWAPO. It is in this context that UNTAG's contribution to the successful administration of the election must be considered.

Assessment of April Events

The Special Representative's decision in April to authorize the release of South African troops from their bases was widely criticized. SWAPO, the OAU and the Frontline states were particularly strident in their condemnation. Ahtisaari, however, apparently believed that the incursion posed a threat to the overall transition process and that he had no choice but to permit the deployment of South African troops.

Critics also questioned the UN's failure to deploy peace-keeping troops by April 1. Even with a full contingent, however, UNTAG could not have prevented the infiltration.

The events of early April substantially disrupted and delayed the timetable for the implementation of the Settlement Plan. SADF troops were not confined to base again until the middle of May. UNTAG civilian officials were not fully deployed in the field until June. Attention was diverted from the critical task of developing the legal framework for the various stages of the election process. More important, criticism of UNTAG's response to the incursion, and the ensuing conflict, eroded confidence, in some quarters, in Ahtisaari and in the Settlement Plan and left UNTAG's subsequent management of the transition process vulnerable to criticism and second-guessing. UNTAG's entire operation never fully recovered from this loss of trust.

Relations between New York and Windhoek

The repercussions from the SR's decision to release South African troops unsettled the environment, which invited even closer scrutiny from the international community and thus from UN headquarters in New York. The Secretary-General formed a high-level task force, which met daily in New York, to advise him about events in Namibia. The task force coordinated communications between the Special Representative and the Secretary-General and tried to supervise developments in Namibia.

The Secretary-General's task force operated under no formal terms of reference and had no exact precedent in UN history, although senior UN officials did meet regularly during the crisis in the Belgian Congo. Task force members worked simply to provide policy and operational guidance to the Secretary-General and the Special Representative. Formation of the task force constituted an effort to coordinate UN policy with respect to Namibia and to ensure that the UN spoke with one voice both to colleagues in the field and to the international community.

On the political level, the task force represented an attempt, after the events of early April, to regain the confidence and support of the African member states for the UNTAG mission. The Secretary-General's creation of the office of Deputy Special Representative for Ambassador Legwaila of Botswana was also responsive to the criticisms of African governments that Ahtisaari's front office needed more African representation. The Secretary-General's actions were timely; failure to recognize and respond to the political problem that the UN faced in Namibia undoubtedly would have substantially damaged future UN peacekeeping and other conflict resolution efforts.

Despite the tremendous geographical distance between New York and Windhoek, the task force maintained constant contact with UNTAG. UN headquarters typically received numerous daily cables from UNTAG in Namibia. Task force members analyzed the incoming cables, considered the information at their meetings and dispatched responses. These communications between New York and Windhoek relayed advice on a whole range of subjects: the status of negotiations, military positions, visiting delegations, incidents of intimidation, daily reports from regional offices, and the like. Most of the communications from Windhoek came from Ahtisaari, but Prem Chand, the military force commander, often reported directly to New York. Most of the task force's communications from New York to Windhoek came from UN Under-Secretary Goulding. The close interaction between the task force and the Special Representative was illustrated during the negotiations over the election law. While the SR understandably sought to establish a cooperative working relationship with the Administrator-General, Ahtisaari's response to the AG's initial versions of the laws governing the electoral process was criticized as too tentative; the proposed laws would have created a system that was unacceptable to the international community. After the AG presented his unacceptable draft of the election law in July, the Secretary-General dispatched Paul Szasz to assist the SR in the negotiating process.

On the other side, some Namibian political party and local government officials, as well as some international observers, lamented Ahtisaari's lack of authority and what was perceived as his apparent caution in making moves without checking with his superiors in New York. This lament amounted to an implicit criticism of UN headquarters in New York for failing to provide more authority to Ahtisaari, an experienced diplomat who was observing the process first-hand. Prem Chand's practice of reporting directly to New York also engendered a few complaints by civilian authorities in Windhoek, and it limited somewhat the military's accountability to the SR.

While the task force presented somewhat of a problem for Ahtisaari, it also increased his leverage. In his dealings with the AG, Ahtisaari could always blame New York for the harder line. Also, when negotiations in Namibia reached a stalemate, the task force would discuss these matters directly with the South African representative in New York. This was true especially of the amnesty law, the registration law and the election law.

Both bureaucratic politics and normal personality clashes seem to have interfered with the relationship between New York and Windhoek. However, it was the difference in perspectives between New York and Windhoek that caused the most difficulty. Especially in the early months of the transition, New York viewed Ahtisaari and his staff as too compliant in dealing with the AG. At the same time, UNTAG personnel in Windhoek saw New York as removed from the reality as it existed in the territory -- too responsive to the demands of the non-aligned movement, the OAU and the Frontline states, and insufficiently oriented toward the real goal, making sure elections were held in a manner consistent with the intent of Resolution 435.

UNTAG Responses to Intimidation Problems

Despite persistent problems of intimidation, the presence of UNTAG military, police and civilian personnel contributed substantially to the maintenance of stability, and ultimately to the reduction of intimidation incidents. CIVPOL's monitoring of SWAPOL and Koevoet discouraged abuses by these territorial security forces. The UN military force contributed to a calmer atmosphere by monitoring the border area and the confinement to base of SADF troops remaining in Namibia.

SWAPOL and CIVPOL officials reported that problems of cooperation were nonexistent between counterparts at the officer level. At lower levels, many SWA policemen seemed to resent CIVPOL's oversight, which they perceived as nitpicking and second-guessing. Nonetheless, in Ovamboland in early October, CIVPOL and SWAPOL created a special anti-intimidation squad and established joint investigation teams. These structures contributed to improved working relationships and a reduction in incidents of intimidation.

UNTAG could perhaps have adopted a more aggressive and uniform policy with respect to the investigation of alleged incidents of intimidation. Many CIVPOL officers felt constrained by their role as monitors. They could only urge victims of intimidation to file reports with SWAPOL, despite the fact that SWAPOL members were often the target of the complaints. At a minimum, UNTAG should have insisted on receiving cooperation from SWAPOL, including more notification as to the schedule of patrols, prompt investigation of referred complaints and access to investigation files.

In the early days of the transition, the UN's response to the ongoing Koevoet problem was inadequate. For months, after the government simply integrated Koevoet into SWAPOL, Koevoet members continued to be the source of many reported incidents of intimidation and assault. The AG finally demobilized Koevoet members in SWAPOL in late September, five weeks before the election. The demobilization only transferred the problem of intimidation, however. Ex-Koevoet members, often wearing DTA colors or hired as DTA party organizers, continued to terrorize and intimidate SWAPO supporters.

In retrospect, many believe that the complete demobilization of Koevoet was a mistake. It would have been preferable, according to these observers, to confine Koevoet units to base outside of Ovamboland, where UNTAG could have closely monitored their activities, and where they could have been retrained for more traditional police duties.

Supervision of Registration and Balloting

UNTAG personnel monitored each registration location and in many cases assisted in registering voters. The registration period provided an opportunity for UNTAG field personnel to prove their operational capabilities, as well as to establish a high profile within the general Namibian population. This experience was repeated and expanded during the balloting process.

Mission to Investigate Allegations of Continuing Detentions

UNTAG did not include within its mandate the investigation of alleged mistreatment of detainees. Only in response to allegations of continued detentions did the UN become involved, and then only belatedly. Its handling of these allegations became one of the most criticized aspects of the operation.

Unfortunately the UN decision to send a survey mission to investigate alleged abuses was made late in the transition process, after the issue had become highly politicized. Further, the mission's failure to include ex-detainees, its inability to broaden its perspective by obtaining the participation of the International Committee for the Red Cross or any other international human rights organization, and its reliance on the cooperation of SWAPO, hurt its credibility, if not its effectiveness. On the other hand, unless the mission had returned with a SWAPO detainee, it would not have satisfied those who sought to use this issue politically.

Role and Impact of Observer Groups

The Special Representative welcomed outside observers from governments and from intergovernmental and nongovernmental organizations. In addition to intergovernmental organizations with permanent missions in Namibia, such as the OAU and the Frontline states, the non-aligned movement and the Commonwealth sent observer groups. A number of nongovernmental organizations also sent observers and commented on the process; these included NDI, Oxfam, the Commission on Namibia of the Lawyers Committee for Civil Rights under Law, the European Parliamentarians Against Apartheid, and various church groups. Certain governments, including the United States, sent high-level observer missions during the election period.

Due to the presence of these observer groups, many complaints of intimidation and criticisms of the proposed laws were aired in public and in diplomatic forums throughout the world. Political parties, normally aggressive critics of proposed elections laws, took a less assertive stance in Namibia; observer groups thus stepped in to play the more critical role.

In presenting their concerns, many of the observer organizations aligned themselves with one or another of the Namibian parties. Moreover, some observer groups either did not accept the legitimacy of Resolution 435 or were constantly urging the UN to rewrite 435 to favor a particular party. In these respects, the observer groups acted inconsistently with recognized standards for international election observing, which mandates neutrality and objectivity. Notwithstanding these criticisms, observer organizations played a largely salutary role.

International Election Standards

As reflected in the negotiating record and the Secretary-General's reports, the development of the Namibian election system provides a basis for analyzing standards for what the international community perceives to be a free and fair electoral process. While the Settlement Plan stated certain criteria explicitly, others evolved from the process of responding to the criticisms of the election system originally proposed by the AG.

Resolution 435 injected substance into the principle of free elections established by the Universal Declaration of Human Rights. Article 21 of the Universal Declaration states that "everyone has the right to take part in the government of his country, directly or through freely chosen representatives." It adds that:

> The will of the people shall be the basis of the authority of government; this will shall be expressed in periodic and genuine elections which shall be by universal and equal suffrage and shall be held by secret vote or by equivalent free voting procedures.

In Namibia, the UN developed and applied standards that moved beyond this limited formula to ensure that the Namibian elections occurred in a free environment with administratively fair rules. The improvements made in the final election law, as compared to the original draft, suggest that the UN can develop a consensus on what constitutes a free and fair election system that goes beyond the political rights provisions included in human rights instruments.

The most important of these standards in the Namibian context were: 1) secrecy of the ballot; 2) reasonable speed in the counting of ballots; and 3) accountability and openness of the process to the competing parties. The UN in effect maintained that universal practice, coupled with the provisions of the international human rights instruments, established these electoral principles under international law.

Future UN Election-Monitoring Operations

The UN may play a major role in future elections, especially elections used for conflict resolution. In addition to the Namibia experience described in this report, the UN recently observed, at the invitation of the government, the February 25 Nicaraguan elections. UN election-related missions have been also discussed in the context of Afghanistan, Cambodia, El Salvador, Romania and Western Sahara.

The United Nations Observer Mission to Verify the Nicaraguan Electoral Process (ONUVEN) was based in the country beginning August 1989, and grew to more than 230 observers present on election day. The Secretary-General appointed as his special representative to the elections former U.S. Attorney General Elliot Richardson, who visited Nicaragua several times during the election period. As part of their verification responsibilties, ONUVEN personnel reviewed the election law, observed the registration process in all regions of the country, monitored the election campaign and prepared in-depth reports on the quality of the election process. Their presence at campaign rallies, together with the presence of their counterparts from the Organization of American States (OAS), was a major factor in reducing the levels of violence and in providing confidence to the population. ONUVEN, the OAS and former U.S. President Jimmy Carter also pressured the government and the election council to adopt changes that improved the election environment.

The large size of the ONUVEN election-day delegation permitted visits to more than 40 percent of the polling sites and an ONUVEN-organized parallel vote tabulation. The latter, by providing a quick and accurate projection of the results, played a significant role in minimizing tensions on elecion night and in assuring that the results would be respected. In the aftermath of the elections, ONUVEN sought to encourage a smooth transition in a country that has never seen a transfer of political power resulting from an election.

The proposed UN roles in Cambodia and Western Sahara are more ambitious than the Nicaragua effort. In the former, a plan has been presented whereby the UN would administer the country in preparation for elections, which would then be supervised by the UN. In the Western Sahara, the UN may be called upon to organize and conduct a referendum to settle the conflict between Morocco and the Polisario Front.

At a political level, the UN operation in Namibia certainly built confidence in the United Nations' capabilities and integrity, and it augurs well for the organization's role in places like Cambodia and the Western Sahara. Given the positive outcome in Namibia, the UN undoubtedly brought much more credibility to fulfilling its role in the Nicaraguan elections. Such accomplishments are likely to spur member states to entrust additional responsibilities to the UN in dealing with regional and even national conflicts.

Although the Namibian operation, like each UN peacekeeping and election-monitoring operation, is unique, there are certainly experiences to share and lessons to learn. Perhaps most important, the UN should consider building an infrastructure for conflict resolution and election monitoring missions that is capable of quickly assuming a responsible role in an appropriate situation. At a minimum, there should exist within the UN an institutional familiarity with election laws and administrative procedures, written training materials on election monitoring and detailed information about previous missions. In addition, interested parties should settle the planning and budgetary battles in sufficient time to avoid hampering implementation. Finally, all sides should be aware that they are expected to keep their commitments and to play by agreed upon understandings.

Chapter 11

REFLECTIONS AND CONCLUSIONS

The Namibian transition has significance far beyond resolution of the status of the last territory mandated by the League of Nations, and even beyond the realization of the aspirations of Namibians for true freedom. Implicated in the process are the future of participatory democracy in Africa, the survival of South Africa's system of minority rule, the prospects for further collaboration between the United States and the Soviet Union in the region, and the capacity of the United Nations to help resolve disputes and assist in nation building. More specifically, to the extent that the international community perceives the UN's efforts with respect to the Namibian elections to be a success, that experience becomes a model for other regions.

For the great majority of people, UNTAG represented a check on abuses by South Africa and the transition government. The men and women with blue armbands or blue berets were visible evidence that the international community was concerned about the welfare of Namibians, that the long-sought cessation of war was not a cruel trick, and that the elections would indeed be free and fair. UNTAG was a powerful symbol and source of hope. That hope became a reality as UNTAG increasingly allayed concerns about intimidation and South Africa's intentions.

In view of the apparent success of the UN operation in Namibia, discussion of UN-supervised or UN-controlled elections as a means of conflict resolution is likely to increase. In considering Namibia as a model for UN involvement in elections, it is important to recognize the combination of factors that made the Namibia situation *sui generis*: the long-standing UN involvement, the intransigence of South Africa, the relationship of the Namibian conflict to larger regional conflicts, the struggle against apartheid within South Africa, and the thaw in East-

West relations, to name a few. Nevertheless, the experience in Namibia demonstrates that a UN mission can help ensure the fair conduct of elections. The accumulated experience will be useful, but the UN must proceed carefully to employ this experience in other situations.

This is a world of rapidly accelerating changes characterized by decolonization, democratization and reduced East-West tensions. Events in Eastern Europe reverberate in Africa and elsewhere in the Third World, and there is a distinct inclination toward multi-party systems and more liberalized economies. Recent events in South Africa, including the legalization of political organizations such as the African National Congress and the release of Nelson Mandela, may also give reason for hope about the situation there. The UN can contribute to such democratization trends if it can demonstrate the capability and find the resources.

Namibia has suffered 23 years of war and decades of oppression. SWAPO and South Africa battled for years on the streets, in the bush, in courtrooms and in the United Nations. But with the help of the United Nations, much of that conflict was redirected into electoral competition.

The Settlement Plan was not just a device for instituting independence; it also helped Namibians develop a democratic system of government, where meaningful elections are held periodically and where human rights are generally respected. To date, the relative harmony of the Constituent Assembly and the adoption of a constitution, which many have called the most liberal in Africa, give reason for optimism.

The timing of this accomplishment will have a real effect on the evolving situation in South Africa. It is difficult to know the extent to which events in Namibia influenced the substance or the timing of President de Klerk's promising actions. What is clear, however, is that a smooth implementation of UN Resolution 435 was an essential precondition of any opening in South Africa.

The recent experience in Namibia suggests that the United Nations played an invaluable and constructive role in ensuring that the elections were free and fair. The full implementation of UN Resolution 435 now allows the Namibian people to express their democratic aspirations through their elected representatives. With a liberal constitution in place, the new nation of Namibia has received as encouraging a beginning as could have been expected. The work of the UN in Namibia represents a major triumph of international cooperation and fulfills the dreams of the UN's founders that it would be an indispensable tool in resolving conflict peacefully.

UNTAG field office in Onekwaya, Ovamboland

NDI Namibia delegation, led by Senator Alisdair Graham, with Martti Ahtisaari, June 6, 1989.

Reception center for exiled returnees in Ongwediva.

SWAPO rally in Ondangwa, June 1989.

Martti Ahtisaari reviews Indian police monitors (CIVPOL) in Caprivi Strip. UN Photo 156734/Milton Grant

Professor Christopher Edley, a member of NDI's June 1989 Namibia delegation, testifies before House Subcommittee on Africa, July 20, 1989.

A military briefing at Sudierhof, UNTAG's military headquarters in Windhoek. Seated left to right, Lt. General Prem Chand, Marrack Goulding, and Martti Ahtisaari. UN Photo 156729/Milton Grant

Rep. Donald Payne visits a registration site in Katutura, July 22, 1989.

Voters line up in Tsumeb on first day of voting, November 7, 1989.

Martti Ahtisaari and Joseph Legwaila visit ballot-counting center at Windhoek showgrounds. UN Photo 157146/Milton Grant

Martti Ahtisaari certifies elections as free and fair, November 14, 1989. UN
Photo 157131/Milton Grant

*NDI Senior Advisory Committee member and chairman of President
Bush's official U.S. Observer Delegation Edmund Muskie visits with
President Sam Nujoma.*

APPENDICES

86

Appendix I

CONSULTATIONS AND MEETINGS

Election Observation Mission: May 29 - June 6, 1989
Study of Campaign Environment: July 20 - July 24, 1989
Election Observation Mission: October 31 - November 16, 1989

UNTAG

Martti Ahtisaari
Special Representative

Nicholas Bwakira
UN High Commissioner for
Refugees

Dewan Prem Chand
Commander
UNTAG Military

Hisham Omayad
Chief Electoral Officer

Legwaila Joseph Legwalia
Deputy Special Representative

Cedric Thornberry
Director
Office of Special
Representative

Steven Fanning
Commander
UNTAG Police Monitoring Unit

Victor Andreev
Regional Director
Windhoek

Patrick Agboda
Coordinator
Civilian Police Unit
Ovamboland

Hugo Anson
Press Spokesman

Oluseyi Bajulaiye
Deputy Head
Civilian Police Unit
Ovamboland

Karen Barret
Public Relations

Hugh Brophy
Electoral Division

B. Akporode Clarke
Representative in Angola
United Nations Mission

Linda Cohen
Regional Director
Rundu

Fred Eckhard
Press Spokesman

Jean Claude Epardeau
District Director
Entengua

Peter Fitzgerald
Commander
Civilian Police Unit
Ovamboland

Hans Glittenberg
Regional Director
Keetmanshoop

Margaret Kelly
Senior Liaison Officer

Anthony Lydon
Regional Director
Khorixas

UNTAG continued

Mikael Magnusson
Deputy Regional Director
Mariental

Geoffrey Mariki
District Director
Gibeon

Blandina Negga
Regional Director
Gobabis

Kwame Opoku
Senior Legal Advisor

Yumos Othman
Col. Malaysian Monitors
Ovamboland

Paavo Pitumen
District Director
Ondangwa

Shirley Perry
District Director
Tsumeb

Hussein Rahim
Regional Director
Gibeon

John Rwambuya
Regional Director
Ovamboland

Mislan Saiman
Col. Commanding Officer
Kenya Monitors
Ovamboland

Mpazi Sinjela
Special Assistant
Deputy Special Representative

Paul Szasz
Senior Legal Advisor

Gennady Tchistov
District Director
Grootfontein

John Truman
Assistant Electoral Officer

Office of the Administrator General

Ben Baytal
Election Director
Rundu

Carl Botha
Secretary of Administration
Rundu

Col. Hans Dreyer
Founder
Koevoet Paramilitary Unit

Sorel Jacobs
Magistrate
Gobabis

Gert Englebrecht
Deputy Chief Registrar

Karl von Hirschburg
Ambassador
Foreign Affairs

Raymond Matthews
Assistant Electoral Officer

Brig. E. Molendorff
Regional Commander
South West African Police
Ovamboland

Geoffrey Mariki
District Head
Gibeon

A.M. Mundt
Acting Secretary of General
    Services
Ovamboland

Appendix I

Office of the Administrator General continued

Dennis Nandi
Secretary of Education
Ovamboland

Louis Pienaar
Administrator General

Gerhard Roux
Official Spokesman

Peter Roux
Press Director

A.G. Visser
Chief Registration Officer

Col. J. Von Tonder
Liaison Officer (UNTAG)
South West African Police
Ovamboland

Political Parties

ACN
  Kosie Pretorius
  Leader

  Jan de Wet
  Leader

DTA
  Dirk Mudge
  Chairman

  Barney Barnes
  Regional Director

  Tal Burges
  Leader
  Rundu

  Aloys Gende
  Leader
  Rundu

  Katuutire Kaura
  Vice President

  Gabriel Kautuima
  Vice President

  Andrew Matjila
  Deputy Chairman

  Mishake Muyongo
  Senior Vice President

  Nico Smit
  Regional Chairman
  Ovamboland

NNF
  Vekuil Rukoro
  President

  Ottilie Abrahams
  Secretary General

  Kenneth Abrahams
  Secretary for Publicity and
    Information

  Nora Chase
  International Secretary

NPF
  Moses Katjiuongua
  Leader

  Urbanus Karamata
  Secretary for Education
    and Culture

  R. Muramgi
  Representative

  John G. Muundjua
  Treasurer

  Tjeripo Ngaringombe
  Vice President
  Secretary of Foreign
    Affairs

Appendix I

Political Parties continued

SWAPO
  Hendrik Witbooi
  Vice President

  Libertine Amadhila
  Deputy Secretary for Health
   and Welfare

  Hage Geingob
  Election Director

  Theo-Ben Gurirab
  International Secretary

  Esra Kakukura
  Rundu

  Joshua Hoebeb
  Former Secretary of Education

Nicki Nashanti
Ovamboland

Eliaken Shiimi
Ondangwa

Danny Tjongarero
Deputy National Chairman

Anton von Wietersheim
Rehoboth

UDF
  Chief Justus Garoeb
  Leader

  Ernest Likando
  Secretary-General

Church Representatives

Matti Amadhila
Evangelical Lutheran Church
Ovamboland

Rally Deffenbaugh
Lawyer
Lutheran Office for World Community

Bishop Kleopas Dumeni
Executive Member
Council of Churches in
  Namibia
Evangelical Lutheran Church

Olof Erickson
Evangelical Lutheran Church
Ovamboland

Hendrik Frederik
Bishop, President
Council of Churches in
  Namibia

J. Issakas
Elder, Lutheran Church
Gibeon

Roger Key
Executive Member
Council of Churches in
  Namibia
Anglican Church

Pastor Lebe
Evangelical Lutheran
  Church
Khorixas

Father Bernard Nordkamp
Executive Member
Council of Churches in
  Namibia
Roman Catholic Church

Father Patrus
Roman Catholic Church
Khorixas

Appendix I

Diplomatic Corps

Richard Chibuwe
Political Counselor, Zimbabwe
Mission of the Frontline States

A.M.D.P. Chongo
Ambassador, Mozambique
Mission of the Frontline States

A.J. Fulilwa
Political Counselor, Zambia
Mission of the Frontline States

Neil Haffey
Head
Canadian Mission

Sam Hanson
Political Counselor
Canadian Mission

P.K. Kanuma
Ambassador, Zambia
Mission of the Frontline States

R. Korosso
Ambassador, Tanzania
Mission of the Frontline States

Roger McGuire
Director
United States Mission

Jane Madden
Political Counselor
Australian Embassy

K.G.D. Manyika
Ambassador, Zimbabwe
Mission of the Frontline States

B.N. Migenge
Ambassador, Zambia
Mission of the Frontline States

Karen Monaghan
Attache
United States Mission

Ami R. Mpungwe
Political Counselor, Tanzania
Mission of the Frontline States

Christopher Musanga
Representative
Mission of the Frontline States

A. Neto
Political Counselor, Angola
Mission of the Frontline States

Botgatsu G. Pilane
Political Counselor, Zambia
Mission of the Frontline States

M.B.L. Phiri
Minister
Malawi Mission

Alberto Ribeiro
Ambassador, Angola
Mission of the Frontline States

O.J. Tebape
Ambassador, Botswana
Mission of the Frontline States

Peter Wallis
Head
British Mission

Nick Warner
Head
Australian Mission

Other Organizations

Nahum Gorelick
Director
Namibia Peace Plan Study and
    Contact Group (NPP 435)

Ambrosio Hamutenya
Legal Assistance Center

Foibe Louise Jacob
Assistant Director
Human Rights Center

Peter Koep
Chairman
Namibia Peace Plan Study
    and Contact Group (NPP 435)

Jeff Lake
Director
Foundation for Democracy

Gwen Lister
Editor, The Namibian

Simon Maruta
Justice and Peace Commission

Des Matthews
President
Chamber of Commerce

Samuel Koavoto Mbambo
National Teachers' Union

Heinrick Mienert
Farmer

Johanna Mweshida
Teacher

Bryan O'Linn
Chairman
Committee for the Prevention of
    Intimidation and Election
    Malpractices

Johan Smits
Businessman

David Smuts
Director
Legal Assistance Center

Fanuel Tjingaete
Economist, Lecturer
University of Namibia

Barnabas Tjizu
General Secretary
Metal Allied Namibia Workers'
    Union (MANWU)

Piet Venter
Chairman and Director
South West African Broadcasting
    Corporation (SWABC)

Four Former SWAPO Detainees
(Names not available)

International Election Observer Delegations

Churches Information and Monitoring Service (CIMS)

Commission on Independence for Namibia

European Parliamentarians Against Apartheid

Diplomatic Observer Mission of the Frontline States

International Federation of Free Trade Unions

Inter-Parliamentary Union

Non-Aligned Movement

Organizations of African States

OXFAM

Socialist International

U.S. Presidential Delegation

World Congress of Trade Unions

Appendix II

Congress of the United States
House of Representatives
United States Senate
Washington, DC

October 24, 1989

The Honorable Walter F. Mondale
Chairman
National Democratic Institute
1717 Massachusetts Avenue, N.W.
Washington, D.C. 20036

Dear Vice President Mondale:

The National Democratic Institute for International Affairs (NDI) has made an important contribution to promoting a free and fair electoral process in Namibia. NDI's August report offered an excellent review of the situation in Namibia and an effective critique of the proposed electoral laws. We note with satisfaction that several of the potential problems identified in the report have been resolved through changes in the election law that was adopted earlier this month.

From your report and the reports of others, we understand that the United Nations is playing an important, and in many ways, unique role in the Namibian election process. This has significance, particularly if the election proceeds in a free and fair manner, for other regions of the world where elections are contemplated as a possible means of resolving long-standing conflicts.

To better understand the role of the United Nations in the Namibian electoral process, we request that NDI prepare a comprehensive report on this subject. The report should focus particular attention on the U.N. operation as it related to the formulation of administrative and legal procedures, to the government and political parties, and to the complaints of election-related intimidation.

Given NDI's knowledge of the Namibian situation and its experience observing elections in countries around the world, we are convinced that an NDI report on this subject would be objective and place in perspective the contribution of the U.N. to the process. Because of our concern with this matter, we would appreciate an immediate report on the U.N. role in monitoring the balloting and counting processes.

We also would request that NDI prepare a more complete
report using the official arrival of the U.N. Transitional
Assistance Group through certification of the election results
as a timeframe.

Sincerely,

Senator John Kerry
Chairman
Subcommittee on Terrorism,
  Narcotics and International
  Operations
Committee on Foreign Relations
United States Senate

Representative Howard Wolpe
Chairman
Subcommittee on Africa
Committee on Foreign Affairs
United States House of
  Representatives

Senator Paul Simon
Chairman
Subcommittee on African Affairs
Committee on Foreign Relations
United States Senate

Representative Gus Yatron
Chairman
Subcommittee on Human Rights
  and International
  Organizations
Committee on Foreign Affairs
United States House of
  Representatives

Appendix III

Namibia: Resolution 431

United Nations

Security Council Resolution 431(1978) of 27 July 1978

The Security Council,

Recalling its resolution 385(1976) of 30 January 1976,

Taking note of the proposal for a settlement of the Namibian situation contained in document S/12636 of 10 April 1978,

1. *Requests* the Secretary-General to appoint a Special Representative for Namibia in order to ensure the early independence of Namibia through free elections under the supervision and control of the United Nations;

2. *Further requests* the Secretary-General to submit at the earliest possible date a report containing his recommendations for the implementation of the proposal in accordance with Security Council resolution 385(1976);

3. *Urges* all concerned to exert their best efforts towards the achievement of independence by Namibia at the earliest possible date.

Namibia: S/12636

Letter (S/12636) dated 10 April 1978 from the Representatives of Canada, France, the Federal Republic of Germany, the United Kingdom of Great Britain and Northern Ireland and the United States of America to the President of the Security Council

On instructions from our Governments we have the honour to transmit to you a proposal for the settlement of the Namibian situation and to request that it should be circulated as a document of the Security Council.

The objective of our proposal is the independence of Namibia in accordance with resolution 385(1976), adopted unanimously by the Security Council on 30 January 1976. We are continuing to work towards the implementation of the proposal.

Proposal for a Settlement of the Namibian Situation

I. Introduction

1. Bearing in mind their responsibilities as members of the Security Council, the Governments of Canada, France, the Federal Republic of Germany, the United Kingdom and the United States have consulted with the various parties involved with the Namibian situation with a view to encouraging agreement on the transfer of authority in Namibia to an independent government in accordance with resolution 385(1976), adopted unanimously by the Security Council on 30 January 1976.

2. To this end, our Governments have drawn up a proposal for the settlement of the Namibian question designed to bring about a transition to independence during 1978 within a framework acceptable to the people of Namibia and thus to the international community. While the proposal addresses itself to all elements of resolution 385(1976), the key to an internationally acceptable transition to independence is free elections for the whole of Namibia as one political entity with an appropriate United Nations role in accordance with resolution 385(1976). A resolution will be required in the Security Council requesting the Secretary-General to appoint a United Nations Special Representative whose central task will be to make sure that conditions are established which will allow free and fair elections and an impartial electoral process. The Special Representative will be assisted by a United Nations Transition Assistance Group.

3. The purpose of the electoral process is to elect representatives to a Namibian Constituent Assembly which will draw up and adopt the Constitution for an independent and sovereign Namibia. Authority would then be assumed during 1978 by the Government of Namibia.

4. A more detailed description of the proposal is contained below. Our Governments believe that this proposal provides an effective basis for implementing resolution 385(1976) while taking adequate account of the interests of all parties involved. In carrying out his responsibilities, the Special Representative will work together with the official appointed by South Africa (the Administrator-General) to ensure the orderly transition to independence. This working arrangement shall in no way constitute recognition of the legality of the South African presence in and administration of Namibia.

II. The Electoral Process

5. In accordance with Security Council resolution 385(1976), free elections will be held, for the whole of Namibia as one political entity, to enable the people of Namibia freely and fairly to determine their own future. The elections will be under the supervision and control of the United Nations in that, as a condition to the conduct of the electoral process, the elections themselves and the certification of their results, the United Nations Special Representative will have to satisfy himself at each stage as to the fairness and appropriateness of all

measures affecting the political process at all levels of administration before such measures take effect.
Moreover the Special Representative may himself make proposals in regard to any aspect of the political process. He will have at his disposal a substantial civilian section of the United Nations Transition Assistance Group (UNTAG) sufficient to carry out his duties satisfactorily. He will report to the Secretary-General, keeping him informed and making such recommendations as he considers necessary with respect to the discharge of his responsibilities. The Secretary-General, in accordance with the mandate entrusted to him by the Security Council, will keep the Council informed.

6. Elections will be held to select a Constituent Assembly which will adopt a Constitution for an independent Namibia. The Constitution will determine the organization and powers of all levels of government. Every adult Namibian will be eligible, without discrimination or fear of intimidation from any source, to vote, campaign and stand for election to the Constituent Assembly. Voting will be by secret ballot, with provisions made for those who cannot read or write. The date for the beginning of the electoral campaign, the date of elections, the electoral system, the preparation of voters rolls, and other aspects of electoral procedures will be promptly decided upon so as to give all political parties and interested persons, without regard to their political views, a full and fair opportunity to organize and participate in the electoral process. Full freedom of speech, assembly, movement and press shall be guaranteed. The official electoral campaign shall commence only after the United Nations Special Representative has satisfied himself as to the fairness and appropriateness of the electoral procedures. The implementation of the electoral process, including the proper registration of voters and the proper and timely tabulation and publication of voting results, will also have to be conducted to the satisfaction of the Special Representative.

7. The following requirements will be fulfilled to the satisfaction of the United Nations Special Representative in order to meet the objective of free and fair elections:

a. Prior to the beginning of the electoral campaign, the Administrator-General will repeal all remaining discriminatory or restrictive laws, regulations, or administrative measures which might abridge or inhibit that objective.

b. The Administrator-General will make arrangements for the release, prior to the beginning of the electoral campaign, of all Namibian political prisoners or political detainees held by the South African authorities

so that they can participate fully and freely in that process, without risk of arrest, detention, intimidation or imprisonment. Any disputes concerning the release of political prisoners or political detainees will be resolved to the satisfaction of the Special Representative acting on the independent advice of a jurist of international standing who will be designated by the Secretary-General to be legal adviser to the Special Representative.

c. All Namibian refugees or Namibians detained or otherwise outside the Territory of Namibia will be permitted to return peacefully and participate fully and freely in the electoral process without risk of arrest, detention, intimidation or imprisonment. Suitable entry points will be designated for these purposes.

d. The Special Representative, with the assistance of the United Nations High Commissioner for Refugees and of other appropriate international bodies, will ensure that Namibians remaining outside of Namibia will be given a free and voluntary choice whether to return. Provision will be made to attest to the voluntary nature of decisions made by Namibians who elect not to return to Namibia.

8. A comprehensive cessation of all hostile acts will be observed by all parties in order to ensure that the electoral process will be free from interference and intimidation. The annex describes provisions for the implementation of the cessation of all hostile acts, military arrangements concerning UNTAG, the withdrawal of South African forces, and arrangements with respect to other organized forces in Namibia, and with respect to the forces of SWAPO. These provisions call for:

a. A cessation of all hostile acts by all parties and the restriction of South African and SWAPO armed forces to base.

b. Thereafter, a phased withdrawal from Namibia of all but 1,500 South African troops within 12 weeks and prior to the official start of the political campaign. The remaining South African force would be restricted to Grootfontein or Oshivello or both and would be withdrawn after the certification of the election.

c. The demobilization of the citizen forces, commandos and ethnic forces, and the dismantling of their command structures.

d. Provision will be made for SWAPO personnel outside the Territory to return peacefully to Namibia through designated entry points to participate freely in the political process.

e. A military section of UNTAG to ensure that the provisions of the agreed solution will be observed by all parties. In establishing the military section of UNTAG, the Secretary-General will keep in mind functional and logistical requirements. The five Governments, as members of the Security Council, will support the Secretary-General's judgement in his discharge of this responsibility. The Secretary-General will, in the normal manner, include in his consultations all those concerned with the implementation of the agreement. The United Nations Special Representative will be required to satisfy himself as to the implementation of all these arrangements and will keep the Secretary-General informed of developments in this regard.

9. Primary responsibility for maintaining law and order in Namibia during the transition period will rest with the existing police forces. The Administrator-General will ensure the good conduct of the police forces to the satisfaction of the United Nations Special Representative and will take the necessary action to ensure their suitability for continued employment during the transition period. The Special Representative will make arrangements, when appropriate, for United Nations personnel to accompany the police forces in the discharge of their duties. The police forces would be limited to the carrying of small arms in the normal performance of their duties.

10. The United Nations Special Representative will take steps to guarantee against the possibility of intimidation or interference with the electoral process from whatever quarter.

11. Immediately after the certification of election results, the Constituent Assembly will meet to draw up and adopt a Constitution for an independent Namibia. It will conclude its work as soon as possible so as to permit whatever additional steps may be necessary prior to the installation of an independent Government of Namibia during 1978.

12. Neighbouring countries will be requested to ensure to the best of their abilities that the provisions of the transitional arrangements, and the outcome of the election, will be respected. They will also be requested to afford the necessary facilities to the United Nations Special Representative and all United Nations personnel to carry out their assigned functions and to facilitate such measures as may be desirable for ensuring tranquillity in the border areas.

Appendix IV

Annex to S/12636

Timing	SAG	SWAPO	UN	Other action
1. At date unspecified:			UNSC passes resolution authorizing SG to appoint UNSR and requesting him to submit plan for UN involvement. SG appoints UNSR and dispatches UN contingency planning group to Namibia. SG begins consultations with potential participants in UNTAG.	
2. As soon as possible, preferably within one week of Security Council action:			SG reports back to UNSC. UNSC passes further resolution adopting plan for UN involvement. Provision is made for financing.	
3. Transitional period formally begins on date of UNSC passage of resolution adopting SG's plan:	General cessation of hostile acts comes under UN supervision. Restriction to base of all South African forces including ethnic forces.	General cessation of hostile acts comes under UN supervision. Restriction to base.	As soon as possible: UNSR and staff (UNTAG) arrive in Namibia to assume duties. UN military personnel commence monitoring of cessation of hostile acts and commence monitoring of both South African and SWAPO troop restrictions. Begin infiltration prevention and border surveillance. Begin monitoring of police forces. Begin monitoring of citizen forces, ethnic forces, and military personnel performing civilian functions. UNSR makes necesary arrangements for co-ordination with neighbouring countries concerning the provisions of the transitional arrangements.	Release of political prisoners/detainees wherever held begins and is to be completed as soon as possible.

4. Within six weeks:	Restriction to base continues. Force levels reduced to 12,000 men.	Restriction to base continues.	Appropriate action by UN High Commissioner for Refugees outside Namibia to assist in return of exiles. All UN activity continues.	Establishment in Namibia of provisions to facilitate return of exiles. Establishment and publication of general rules for elections.
				Completion of repeal of discriminatory laws and restrictive legislation. Dismantlement of command structures of citizen forces, commandos and ethnic forces, including the withdrawal of all South African soldiers attached to these units. All arms, military equipment, and ammunition of citizen forces and commandos confined to drill halls under UN supervision. AG to ensure that none of these forces will drill or constitute an organized force during the transitional period except under order of the AG with the concurrence of UNSR. AG with concurrence of UNSR determines whether and under what circumstances those military personnel performing civilian functions will continue those functions.
5. Within nine weeks:	Restriction to base continues. Force levels reduced to 8,000 men.	Restriction to base continues. Peaceful repatriation under UN supervision starts for return through designated entry points.	All UN activity continues.	Completion of release of political prisoners/detainees wherever held.
6. Within 12 weeks:	Force levels reduced to 1,500 men, restricted to Grootfontein or Oshivello or both. All military installations along northern border would by now either be deactivated or put under civilian control under UN supervision. Facilities which depend on them (e.g. hospitals, power stations) would be protected where necessary by the UN.	Restriction to base continues.	All UN activity continues. Military section of UNTAG at maximum deployment.	

Appendix IV

7. Start of thir-teenth week:			Official start of election campaign of about four months' duration.
8. On date established by AG to satisfac-tion of UNSR:			Election to Constituent Assembly.
9. One week after date of cer-tification of election:	Completion of withdrawal.	Closure of all bases.	Convening of Constituent Assembly.
10. At date unspecified:			Conclusion of Constituent Assembly and whatever additional steps may be necessary prior to in-stallation of new government.
11. By 31 December 1978 at latest:			Independence.

AG = Administrator-General
SAG = South African Government
SG = Secretary-General of the United Nations
SWAPO = South West Africa People's Organization
UN = United Nations
UNSC = United Nations Security Council
UNSR = United Nations Special Representative
UNTAG = United Nations Transition Assistance Group

Namibia: S/12827

United Nations

Report of the Secretary-General (S/12827) Submitted pursuant to Paragraph 2 of Security Council Resolution 431(1978) concerning the Situation in Namibia, 29 August 1978

Introduction

1. At its 2082nd meeting on 27 July 1978, the Security Council adopted resolution 431(1978). By that resolution, the Council, recalling its resolution 385(1976) and taking note of the proposal for a settlement of the Namibian situation contained in document S/12636 of 10 April 1978, requested me to appoint a Special Representative for Namibia in order to ensure the early independence of Namibia through free elections under the supervision and control of the United Nations. The full text of resolution 431(1978) reads as follows:

"*The Security Council,*

Recalling its resolution 385(1976) of 30 January 1976,

Taking note of the proposal for a settlement of the Namibian situation contained in document S/12636 of 10 April 1978.

1. *Requests* the Secretary-General to appoint a Special Representative for Namibia in order to ensure the early independence of Namibia through free elections under the supervision and control of the United Nations;

2. *Further requests* the Secretary-General to submit at the earliest possible date a report containing his recommendations for the implementation of the proposal for a settlement of the Namibian situation in accordance with Security Council resolution 385(1976);

3. *Urges* all concerned to exert their best efforts towards the achievement of independence by Namibia at the earliest possible date."

2. Immediately following the decision of the Council. I appointed Mr. Martti Ahtisaari, the United Nations Commissioner for Namibia, my Special Representative for the purposes of the resolution.

3. Mindful of the Council's further request contained in paragraph 2. I requested my Special Representative to undertake, at the earliest possible date, a survey mission to Namibia for the purpose of gathering for me all the information necessary for the preparation of the present report. To assist him in this task, I placed at his disposal a team of United Nations officials and military advisers.

4. This report, which is based on the survey of my Special Representative, is submitted to the Security Council pursuant to paragraph 2 of resolution 431(1978), in which the Council requested the Secretary-General " to submit at the earliest possible date a report containing his recommendations for the implementation of the proposal in accordance with Security Council resolution 385(1976)".

I. The Survey Mission

5. As stated above, my Special Representative, accompanied by a staff of United Nations officials and military advisers, visited Namibia from 6 to 22 August for the purpose of carrying out a survey of all matters relative to the implementation of resolution 431(1978).

6. In addition to meetings with the Administrator-General of the Territory and his staff, as well as with the South African military and police commanders and local authorities, the Special Representative had the opportunity to consult extensively representatives of political parties, churches, the business community and individuals. His consultations in this regard covered a wide spectrum of public opinion within the Territory. In this connection, the Special Representative and his staff, by travelling extensively within the Territory, were able to familiarize themselves with local conditions which would have relevance to the effective organization and operation of a United Nations Transition Assistance Group (UNTAG) entrusted with the tasks set out in the proposal for a settlement of the Namibian situation contained in document S/12636.

7. In the course of his meetings and consultations, the Special Representative was able to obtain the views of not only the Administrator-General and his staff but also the representatives of the Namibian people on a broad range of important topics relating to the necessary conditions for the holding of free and fair elections and to the role of the United Nations. Among the principal subjects discussed were: the repeal of all the remaining discriminatory or restrictive laws, regulations or administrative measures which might abridge or inhibit the

objective of free and fair elections; arrangements for ensuring the release of political prisoners and detainees, as
well as the voluntary return of Namibians: the arrangements and dispositions required to ensure the cessation of all hostile acts: the electoral process: the composition and work of the Constituent Assembly; and the
timetable for the accomplishment of the above stages.
The military aspects of the operation, with special
reference to the introduction and functioning of the
military component of UNTAG, were also fully
discussed. In addition, the Special Representative also
discussed with the Administrator-General the manner of
ensuring the good conduct of the police and the arrangements necessary to assure the free and unrestricted
discharge by the United Nations staff of the tasks
assigned to them.

II. General Guidelines

8. The implementation of the proposal in paragraph 2
of resolution 431(1978) will require the establishment of
a United Nations Transition Assistance Group in the Territory, consisting of a civilian component and a military
component. Because of the unique character of the
operation and the need for close co-operation between
them, both components will be under the over-all direc-
tion of the Special Representative of the Secretary-
General.

9. The Special Representative will report to me, keeping me informed and making such recommendations as
he considers necessary with respect to the discharge of
his responsibilities. The Secretary-General, in accordance
with the mandate entrusted to him by the Security Council. will keep the Council fully informed of
developments relating to the implementation of the proposal and to the functioning of UNTAG. All matters
which might affect the nature or the continued effective
functioning of UNTAG will be referred to the Council for
its decision.

10. The deployment of both components of UNTAG
must take into account the specific geographic.
demographic, economic and social conditions prevailing
in Namibia. These include, in particular, the vast
distances and varied nature of topography and vegetation;
the broad ranges of climatic conditions; the scarcity of
water; the population distribution and existing communication network, the distribution and concentration of
ethnic groups; and the lack of an adequate infrastructure
in the north, such as roads and other communications
and facilities. All these factors, when analysed, make it
evident that sizeable resources, both military and

civilian, will be required to provide the close monitoring
called for in document S/12636.

11. In performing its functions, UNTAG will act with
complete impartiality. In order that the proposal may be
effectively implemented, it is expected that the
Administrator-General and all other officials from within
the Territory will exhibit the same impartiality.

12. For UNTAG to carry out all its tasks effectively,
three essential conditions must be met. First, it must at
all times have the full support and backing of the
Security Council. Secondly, it must operate with the full
co-operation of all the parties concerned, particularly
with regard to the comprehensive cessation of all hostile
acts. Thirdly, it must be able to operate as a combined
United Nations operation, of which the military component will constitute an integrated, efficient formation
within the wider framework of UNTAG.

13. To monitor the cessation of hostilities effectively, to
maintain surveillance of the Territory's vast borders and
to monitor the restriction to base of the armed forces of
the parties concerned, the co-operation and support of
the neighbouring countries will be necessary. Such co-
operation will be most important, particularly during the
early stages.

14. Implementation of the proposal, and thus the work
of UNTAG, will have to proceed in successive stages.
These stages, which are detailed in the annex to document S/12636, can be grouped as follows:

   a. Cessation of all hostile acts by all parties and
the withdrawal, restriction or demobilization of the
various armed forces;

   b. Conduct of free and fair elections to the Constituent Assembly, for which the pre-conditions include the
repeal of discriminatory or restrictive laws, regulations
or administrative measures, the release of political
prisoners and detainees and voluntary return of exiles,
the establishment of effective monitoring by the United
Nations and an adequate period for electoral campaigning;

   c. The formulation and adoption of a Constitution
for Namibia by the Constituent Assembly;

   d. The entry into force of the Constitution and the
consequent achievement of independence of Namibia.

15. The length of time required for these stages is
directly related to the complexity of the tasks to be performed and to the overriding consideration that certain
steps are necessary before it can be said that elections
have been held under free and fair conditions. It will be
recalled that the proposal envisaged a series of successive stages, spaced so as to provide a sufficient lapse

of time before the holding of the elections. This should permit, among other things, the release of political prisoners and detainees, the return and registration of all Namibians outside the Territory who may wish to participate in the electoral process, the deployment of United Nations military and civilian personnel and electoral campaigning by all parties in an atmosphere of tranquillity. The timetable set out in the proposal called for the lapse of approximately seven months from the date of the approval of the present report by the Security Council to the holding of the elections.

16. In his discussions with the Special Representative, the Administrator-General said that the South African authorities, having previously established 31 December 1978 as the date of independence, felt that they were committed thereto and that, consequently, the elections should take place as scheduled, regardless of the fact that it would necessitate substantially reducing the timetable necessary for completion of the preparatory plans. A majority of the political parties was of the opinion, however, that it was essential to maintain the orderly phasing of the preparatory stages and to allow sufficient time for electoral campaigning in order to ensure free and fair elections. Further, it was pointed out that the actual date of independence would fall within the competence of the Constituent Assembly.

17. It will be recalled however that, at the time the proposal was first formulated, the date of 31 December 1978 was consistent with completion of these steps. The delay in reaching agreement among the parties now makes completion by this date impossible. It is therefore recommended that the transitional period should begin on the date of approval of the present report by the Security Council and proceed in accordance with the steps outlined in document S/12636. Using the same timetable that earlier provided the 31 December 1978 date, an appropriate date for elections would be approximately seven months from the date of the approval of the present report.

18. Estimates of the periods of time required for completion of stages a and b of paragraph 14 above are included in the annex to document S/12636. In view of the fact that the periods required for stages c and d would be determined by the Constituent Assembly, it is expected that the duration of UNTAG would be one year, depending on the date of independence to be decided by the Constituent Assembly.

19. UNTAG will have to enjoy the freedom of movement and communication and other facilities that are necessary for the performance of its tasks. For this purpose UNTAG and its personnel must necessarily have all the relevant privileges and immunities provided for by the Convention on the Privileges and Immunities of the United Nations, as well as those especially required for the proposed operation.

20. The military component of UNTAG will not use force except in self-defence. Self-defence will include resistance to attempts to prevent it from discharging its duties under the mandate of the Security Council. UNTAG will proceed on the assumption that all the parties concerned will co-operate with it and take all the necessary steps for compliance with the decisions of the Council.

III. Establishment of UNTAG

A. Military Component

21. The functions which will be performed by the military component of UNTAG are set out in paragraph 8 and in the annex of document S/12636. These include, in particular:

   a. Monitoring the cessation of hostile acts by all parties, the restriction of South African and SWAPO armed forces to base, the phased withdrawal of all except the specified number of South African forces and the restriction of the remainder to specified locations;

   b. Prevention of infiltration as well as surveillance of the borders of the Territory;

   c. Monitoring the demobilization of citizen forces, commandos and ethnic forces, and the dismantling of their command structure.

22. The military component will assist and support the civilian component of UNTAG in the discharge of its tasks.

23. The military component of UNTAG will be under the command of the United Nations, vested in the Secretary-General, under the authority of the Security Council. The command in the field will be exercised by a Commander appointed by the Secretary-General with the consent of the Council. The Commander will report through the Special Representative to the Secretary-General on all matters concerning the functioning of the military component of UNTAG.

24. The military component will comprise a number of contingents to be provided by Member States upon the request of the Secretary-General. The contingents will be selected in consultation with the Security Council and with the parties concerned, bearing in mind the accepted principle of equitable geographical representation.

dition, a body of selected officers to act as monitors will form an integral part of the military component.

25. The military component, including the monitors, will be provided with weapons of a defensive character, consistent with the guidelines set out in paragraph 20 above.

26. In order that the military component may fulfil its responsibilities, it is considered that it should have a strength of the order of seven infantry battalions, totalling approximately 5,000, plus 200 monitors, and, in addition, command, communications, engineer, logistic and air support elements totalling approximately 2,300. The infantry battalions should be fully self-sufficient.

27. It will be essential to establish an adequate logistic and command system at the very outset of the operation. It will therefore be necessary to obtain urgently from Governments the elements of such a system. In this connection, it may well be necessary to use also the services of civilian contractors for some logistic functions, as appropriate. In the nature of the physical circumstances pertaining to this operation, UNTAG may have to rely to a considerable extent on existing military facilities and installations in Namibia.

B. Civilian Component

28. The civilian component will consist of two elements. One of these elements will be the civil police, whose function will be to assist the Special Representative in implementing the tasks set out in paragraphs 9 and 10 of document S/12636.

29. The duties of the civil police element of UNTAG will include taking measures against any intimidation or interference with the electoral process from whatever quarter, accompanying the existing police forces, when appropriate, in the discharge of their duties and assisting in the realization of the function to be discharged by the Administrator-General to the satisfaction of the Special Representative of ensuring the good conduct of the existing police forces.

30. In order that the UNTAG police may fulfil their responsibilities, as described above, it is considered, as a preliminary estimate, that approximately 360 experienced police officers will be required. It is hoped that police officers will be made available by Governments on a secondment basis, bearing in mind the accepted principle of equitable geographical representation as well as the language and other requirements of the assignment.

31. The non-police element of the civilian component of UNTAG will have the function of assisting the Special Representative in implementing paragraphs 5 to 7 of document S/12636 and the relevant sections of the annex thereto. These tasks will consist, in particular, of the following:

a. Supervising and controlling all aspects of the electoral process, considering the fairness and appropriateness of the electoral procedures, monitoring the balloting and the counting of votes, in order to ensure that all procedures will be strictly complied with, and receiving and investigating complaints of fraud or challenges relating to the electoral process;

b. Advising the Special Representative as to the repeal of discriminatory or restrictive laws, regulations or administrative measures which may abridge or inhibit the objective of free and fair elections;

c. Ensuring the absence of or investigating complaints of intimidation, coercion or restrictions on freedom of speech, movement or peaceful political assembly which may impede the objective of free and fair elections;

d. Assisting in the arrangements for the release of all Namibian political prisoners or detainees and for the peaceful, voluntary return of Namibian refugees or Namibians detained or otherwise outside the Territory;

e. Assisting in any arrangements which may be proposed by the Special Representative to the Administrator-General and implemented by the Administrator-General to the Special Representative's satisfaction intended to inform and instruct the electorate as to the significance of the election and the procedures for voting.

32. Bearing in mind the vast size of the Territory, the dispersal of the population and the lack of adequate communications, it is considered, as a preliminary estimate, that approximately 300 Professional officers, as well as the necessary supporting staff, will be required initially until the cessation of hostile acts has been achieved. Thereafter about 1,000 Professional and 200 Field Service and General Service staff will be required during the electoral campaign and the period of balloting in order to cover all the polling stations. The staff will, among other duties, be required for 24 regional centres and more than 400 polling stations.

33. It is anticipated that some of these officials will be provided from among existing United Nations staff and that some will be persons appointed specially for this operation. In addition, it is my hope that a significant number of officials can be seconded or loaned by Governments. All such seconded or loaned personnel will be required to assume the responsibilities incumbent on United Nations officials.

34. It is also my intention to conduct consultations concerning the designation of a jurist of international standing whose appointment as legal adviser to the Special Representative is provided for in paragraph 7b of document S/12636.

IV. Proposed Plan of Action

35. Subject to the approval of the present report by the Security Council, it is my intention to initiate the operation as quickly as possible.

36. It is my intention to appoint Major-General Hannes Philipp Commander of the military component of UNTAG; he has extensive experience of United Nations peace-keeping operations and is already familiar with the situation in Namibia.

37. Immediately following such a decision by the Security Council, the Special Representative, accompanied by the Commander of the military component, the key elements of their staffs and the essential command and logistic elements, will proceed to Namibia in order to establish the headquarters of UNTAG and begin operations as quickly as possible.

38. A number of Governments have already expressed their interest in providing military contingents for UNTAG. Immediately upon the approval of the present report by the Security Council, it is my intention to consult the Council and the parties concerned on the composition of the military component, bearing in mind the principle of equitable geographical representation, on the one hand, and the necessity of obtaining self-sufficient units, on the other. Every effort will be made to begin the deployment of the military component within three weeks and to bring it to its full strength within 12 weeks. For this to be achieved, it will be necessary to determine the composition of the military component at the earliest possible time.

39. It is also my intention to approach Governments to provide military personnel to serve as monitors. In the initial stages, given the urgency of deploying at least some of the monitors, it may be possible to draw upon officers already serving with other existing United Nations operations. This may also apply to key staff positions.

40. As regards civilian personnel, it is likewise my intention, as stated in paragraphs 30 and 33 above, to approach Governments to make available on secondment or loan experienced police officers to serve as police monitors and other experienced officials to serve in the civilian component of UNTAG. In recruiting civilian staff for UNTAG, I shall bear in mind both the accepted principle of equitable geographical representation and the urgent need to deploy a large number of experienced staff within the shortest possible time.

V. Financial Implications

41. At present there are too many unknown factors to permit an accurate assessment of the cost of UNTAG. Based on the numbers of personnel specified in this report and the envisaged duration of 12 months, and taking into account the magnitudes and elements of the financial requirements experienced in other peace-keeping operations, the indications are that the financial requirements for UNTAG could be as high as $300 million, of which approximately $33 million will be required to finance the return of refugees and exiles. In view of the nature of the operation, due regard should be given to the fact that some elements of the operation may be phased out before the end of the mandate and that alternative arrangements may be possible which could result in lower costs.

42. The costs of UNTAG shall be considered expenses of the Organization to be borne by the Member States in accordance with Article 17, paragraph 2, of the Charter.

Appendix IV

Namibia: S/12869

United Nations

Explanatory Statement by the Secretary-General (S/12869) regarding his Report Submitted pursuant to Paragraph 2 of Security Council Resolution 431(1978) concerning the Situation in Namibia (S/12827), 29 September 1978

It is now one month since I submitted to the Security Council my report (S/12827) on the implementation of the proposal of the Five. During that time, exhaustive studies of my report have been undertaken by the parties concerned and I and my staff have conducted intensive consultations with them. These have revealed a number of concerns regarding which I believe it would be useful if I gave an explanation of the way in which the Special Representative would carry out his mandate. My recommendations are based on the tasks which the proposal contained in document S/12636 of 10 April 1978 explicitly mandated the United Nations Transition Assistance Group (UNTAG) to perform. Were we to follow any other course, these tasks could not be credibly performed.

Concern has been expressed by some members of the Security Council over the cost of this exercise. I recognize that this is a particularly heavy burden for Members to bear and of course I shall try to ensure that the mandate will be carried out in the most economical manner possible. All Members will recognize, however, that the most important consideration is the ability of UNTAG successfully to carry out the tasks assigned to it in the proposal. In the absence of a credible United Nations presence, incidents might take place, intentionally or otherwise, that might lead to a resumption of hostilities. Clearly this would vitiate the whole purpose of UNTAG, which is to ensure that elections will take place freely and fairly in conditions of peace.

I should also like to make some observations about the buildup of the military component of UNTAG. When my Special Representative, accompanied by advisers, visited Namibia, his military adviser, Major-General Philipp, was given access to the military installations in the country, and he was able to hold detailed discussions with the South African military on the local conditions in relation to the tasks which the UNTAG military component will have to take up in order to fulfil the mandate. The part of my report on this subject is, of course, an estimate. It is an estimate based upon reliable professional judgement and experience in the light of the tasks

to be performed and of previous United Nations experience as well as the rules and regulations governing the deployment of United Nations personnel. The military component of UNTAG will be built up gradually and will be introduced, for practical as well as other reasons, by stages. The figure of 7,500 men—which includes 2,300 for logistics—would be the authorized upper limit of the military component, and it is obvious that its actual size at any given time will depend upon the development of the general situation, which I shall keep under constant review, undertaking such consultations as may be necessary. Such factors as the co-operation extended by the parties, the maintenance of cease-fire and the security situation will obviously be very important in this regard. I am also studying means by which at least some of the logistic functions of the military component can be carried out by civilian agencies.

I should also like to make some observations about the procedure by which such United Nations military components are constituted. Although I and my staff have obviously made very informal and preliminary moves to prepare for the task which may be assigned to us by the Security Council, I wish to stress here that no commitments concerning military contingents have been made. Nor could such commitments be made in view of the statement in my report to the Council that "the contingents will be selected in consultation with the Security Council and with the parties concerned, bearing in mind the accepted principle of equitable geographical representation". I wish to emphasize here that in the past this process of consultation has been successfully undertaken, thereby ensuring the co-operation of all parties, without which such an enterprise cannot be successful.

The objective of the United Nations under Security Council resolution 431(1978) is the supervision and control of the entire electoral process. My Special Representative has also to satisfy himself that conditions are established which will allow free and fair elections and an impartial electoral process.

But before the electoral process can begin, it is necessary that conditions should be such that they will facilitate it. According to the proposal set out in document S/12636. a general cessation of hostile acts will take place immediately after the Security Council has passed a resolution approving my report. In this connection, I note that the South West Africa People's Organization and South Africa have each indicated their willingness to observe a cease-fire provided the other does the same. As I have stated in my report, and as is clearly envisaged in paragraphs 4 and 12 of the proposal, the co-operation of all concerned is essential to the success of UNTAG. I welcome the assurances I have received from the neighbouring States, and I intend to instruct my Special Representative, as soon as my report is adopted, to explore with them practical ways to facilitate his task.

In paragraphs 29 and 30 of my report I intended to indicate how the Special Representative would fulfil his responsibilities concerning the existing police. According to document S/12636, primary responsibility for maintaining law and order in Namibia during the transition period shall rest with the existing police. However, the Special Representative is also given explicit responsibilities:

a. To satisfy himself that the Administrator-General ensures the good conduct of the police force;

b. To satisfy himself that the Administrator-General takes the necessary action to ensure the suitability of the police for continued employment during the transition period;

c. To make arrangements when appropriate for United Nations personnel to accompany the police forces in the discharge of their duties.

It was therefore necessary to have designated personnel at the disposal of the Special Representative to ensure that these monitoring responsibilities would be satisfactorily performed. Moreover, I concluded that, for reasons of safety and effectiveness, these tasks would best be performed by civilian personnel who were professionally qualified. Concern has also been expressed as to whether the number of United Nations personnel to monitor the police is appropriate to the tasks they are expected to perform. I shall of course keep this question under continuous review.

A number of considerations have been raised regarding the timing of elections and the date of independence for Namibia. As indicated in my report, a majority of the political parties is of the opinion that it is essential to maintain the orderly phases of the preparatory stages and to allow sufficient time for electoral campaigning in order to ensure free and fair elections. Surely, the objective is not simply the holding of elections by a certain date, but the holding of elections which are manifestly free and fair.

It is essential that all aspects of the electoral process should be beyond reproach and, equally important, that this should be apparent. Various parties have expressed concern over the process of registration for elections, and a number of complaints about the existing registration have been brought to my notice. The proposal makes clear that at each stage of the entire electoral process the Special Representative must satisfy himself as to the fairness and appropriateness of all measures affecting the political process at all levels of administration before such measures take effect.

Clearly, therefore, the Special Representative, on arrival in the Territory, will look afresh at all the processes and measures, including the registration of voters, in order to satisfy himself that these are fair and appropriate. Accordingly, the Special Representative will review the registration process, and I can assure all parties that no registration process will receive his approval until he is fully satisfied as to its fairness. In accordance with paragraph 10 of document S/12636, the Special Representative will take steps to guarantee against the possibility of intimidation or interference with the electoral process from whatever quarter.

In conclusion, I should like to emphasize once again that the implementation of my report will depend on the co-operation and understanding of all the parties concerned, and of course of all members of the Security Council. In this connection, I am glad to note that the five Western Governments have given me full assurances of their continued good offices to facilitate the implementation of the report. To this end, my Special Representative will also conduct such further consultations as are deemed necessary. I also trust that the clarifications which I have just given will serve to meet the concerns of all the parties.

Appendix IV

Namibia: Resolution 435

United Nations

Security Council Resolution 435(1978) of 29 Sepember 1978

The Security Council,

Recalling its resolutions 385(1976) of 30 January 1976 and 431(1978) and 432(1978) of 27 July 1978,

Having considered the report submitted by the Secretary-General pursuant to paragraph 2 of resolution 431(1978) (S/12827) and his explanatory statement made in the Security Council on 29 September 1978 (S/12869),

Taking note of the relevant communications from the Government of South Africa addressed to the Secretary-General,

Taking note also of the letter dated 8 September 1978 from the President of the South West Africa People's Organization (SWAPO) addressed to the Secretary-General (S/12841),

Reaffirming the legal responsibility of the United Nations over Namibia.

1. *Approves* the report of the Secretary-General (S/12827) for the implementation of the proposal for a settlement of the Namibian situation (S/12636) and his explanatory statement (S/12869);

2. *Reiterates* that its objective is the withdrawal of South Africa's illegal administration of Namibia and the transfer of power to the people of Namibia with the assistance of the United Nations in accordance with resolution 385(1976);

3. *Decides* to establish under its authority a United Nations Transition Assistance Group (UNTAG) in accordance with the above-mentioned report of the Secretary-General for a period of up to 12 months in order to assist his Special Representative to carry out the mandate conferred upon him by paragraph 1 of Security Council resolution 431(1978), namely, to ensure the early independence of Namibia through free and fair elections under the supervision and control of the United Nations;

4. *Welcomes* SWAPO's preparedness to co-operate in the implementation of the Secretary-General's report, including its expressed readiness to sign and observe the cease-fire provisions as manifested in the letter from the President of SWAPO dated 8 September 1978 (S/12841);

5. *Calls on* South Africa forthwith to co-operate with the Secretary-General in the implementation of this resolution;

6. *Declares* that all unilateral measures taken by the illegal administration in Namibia in relation to the electoral process, including unilateral registration of voters, or transfer of power, in contravention of Security Council resolutions 385(1976), 431(1978) and this resolution, are null and void;

7. *Requests* the Secretary-General to report to the Security Council no later than 23 October 1978 on the implementation of this resolution.

1989 Namibian Election Results

Party Affiliation	Seats Won	Total Votes	Pct. of Vote
Aksie Christelik Nasionaal (ACN)	3	23,728	3.537
Christian Democratic Action			
for Social Justice (CDA)	0	2,495	0.372
Democratic Turnhalle Alliance (DTA)			
Van Namibie	21	191,532	28.551
Federal Convention of Namibia (FCN)	1	10,452	1.558
Namibia National Democratic Party			
(NNDP)	0	984	0.147
Namibia National Front (NNF)	1	5,344	0.797
National Patriotic Front of Namibia			
(NPF)	1	10,693	1.594
South West Africa People's			
Organization (SWAPO)—Democrats			
(SWAPO-D)	0	3,161	0.471
South West Africa People's			
Organization (SWAPO)	41	384,567	57.327
United Democratic Front of Namibia			
(UDF)	4	37,874	5.646
TOTAL	72	670,830	100.00

PRESS
RELEASE

STATEMENT BY MR. MARTTI AHTISAARI,
SPECIAL REPRESENTATIVE OF THE SECRETARY-GENERAL FOR NAMIBIA
TUESDAY, 14 NOVEMBER 1989, 20.00 HOURS

It is my responsibility, under the United Nations' Settlement Plan, to assess the propriety of the electoral process, which has just been completed, for a Constituent Assembly which will draw up and adopt the Constitution for an independent and sovereign Namibia.

Earlier this evening, the Administrator-General informed me of the final results of the election. I have considered all aspects of the process, with particular reference to proper and timely tabulation and publication of voting results, as required by the Security Council.

Revised final returns show that over 97% of Namibians who were registered to vote took the opportunity to exercise their long-awaited and fundamental democratic right. Only a very small fraction of ballots - 1.4% - had to be rejected as invalid, with the concurrence of UNTAG, and under its scrutiny.

Its youngest democracy has given the whole world a shining lesson in democracy; exemplary as to commitment, restraint and tolerance. Accordingly, in this election, there have been no losers: - the whole people of Namibia have been victorious, united in their dedication to peace, reconciliation and the future.   I am sure that Namibians will continue to maintain these admirable qualities during the next days, and I should like to appeal for the maximum restraint and calm at this time.

I have spent many hours at the count here in Windhoek, as has the Administrator-General. The immensely conscientious attention given to each single ballot-paper by a most professional staff, from the United Nations and from Advocate Pienaar's administration, has deeply impressed all who have observed the process of counting and tabulation. My staff throughout the country have reported similar care and accuracy at each stage since the close of voting last Saturday. I wish to express UNTAG's appreciation for the endeavours of all concerned during long, sleepless hours, days and nights. This part of the process has also been a model of proficiency.

A few minutes ago, I informed the Administrator-General, after the establishment of the final results, that I was satisfied with the post-polling procedures that UNTAG has supervised and controlled.

In fulfilment of my responsibility under paragraph 6 of the Proposal for a Settlement of the Namibian Situation, and in accordance with Security Council Resolution 435 of 1978, I hereby certify that the electoral process in Namibia has at each stage been free and fair, and that it has been conducted to my satisfaction.

S

S/RES/385 (1976)
30 January 1976

RESOLUTION 385 (1976)

Adopted by the Security Council at its 1885th meeting, on 30 January 1976

The Security Council,

Having heard the statement by the President of the United Nations Council for Namibia,

Having considered the statement by Mr Moses M Garoeb, Administrative Secretary of the South West Africa People's Organization (SWAPO),

Recalling General Assembly resolution 2145 (XXI) of 27 October 1966, which terminated South Africa's mandate over the Territory of Namibia, and resolution 2248 (S-V) of 19 May 1967, which established a United Nations Council for Namibia, as well as all other subsequent resolutions on Namibia, in particular, resolution 3295 (XXIX) of 13 December 1974 and resolution 3399 (XXX) of 26 November 1975,

Recalling Security Council resolutions 245 (1968) of 25 January and 246 (1968) of 14 March 1968, 264 (1969) of 20 March and 269 (1969) of 12 August 1969, 276 (1970) of 30 January, 282 (1970) of 23 July, 283 (1970) and 284 (1970) of 29 July 1970, 300 (1971) of 12 October and 301 (1971) of 20 October 1971, 310 (1972) of 4 February 1972 and 366 (1974) of 17 December 1974,

Recalling the advisory opinion of the International Court of Justice of 21 June 1971 that South Africa is under obligation to withdraw its presence from the Territory,

Reaffirming the legal responsibility of the United Nations over Namibia,

Concerned at South Africa's continued illegal occupation of Namibia and its persistent refusal to comply with resolutions and decisions of the General Assembly and the Security Council, as well as with the advisory opinion of the International Court of Justice of 21 June 1971,

Gravely concerned at South Africa's brutal repression of the Namibian people and its persistent violation of their human rights, as well as its efforts to destroy the national unity and territorial integrity of Namibia, and its aggressive military build-up in the area,

Strongly deploring the militarization of Namibia by the illegal occupation régime of South Africa,

1. *Condemns* the continued illegal occupation of the Territory of Namibia by South Africa;
2. *Condemns* the illegal and arbitrary application by South Africa of racially discriminatory and repressive laws and practices in Namibia;
3. *Condemns* the South African military build-up in Namibia and any utilization of the Territory as a base for attacks on neighbouring countries;
4. *Demands* that South Africa put an end forthwith to its policy of bantustans and the so-called homelands aimed at violating the national unity and the territorial integrity of Namibia;
5. *Further condemns* South Africa's failure to comply with the terms of Security Council resolution 366 (1974) of 17 December 1974;
6. *Further condemns* all attempts by South Africa calculated to evade the clear demand of the United Nations for the holding of free elections under United Nations supervision and control in Namibia;
7. *Declares* that in order that the people of Namibia be enabled to freely determine their own future, it is imperative that free elections under the supervision and control of the United Nations be held for the whole of Namibia as one political entity;
8. *Further declares* that in determining the date, timetable and modalities for the elections in accordance with paragraph 7 above, there shall be adequate time to be decided upon by the Security Council for the purposes of enabling the United Nations to establish the necessary machinery within Namibia to supervise and control such elections, as well as to enable the people of Namibia to organize politically for the purpose of such elections;
9. *Demands* that South Africa urgently make a solemn declaration accepting the foregoing

provisions for the holding of free elections in Namibia under United Nations supervision and control, undertaking to comply with the resolutions and decisions of the United Nations and with the advisory opinion of the International Court of Justice of 21 June 1971 in regard to Namibia, and recognizing the territorial integrity and unity of Namibia as a nation;

10. *Reiterates its demand* that South Africa take the necessary steps to effect the withdrawal, in accordance with resolutions 264 (1969), 269 (1969) and 366 (1974), of its illegal administration maintained in Namibia and to transfer power to the people of Namibia with the assistance of the United Nations;

11. *Demands* again that South Africa, pending the transfer of powers provided for in the preceding paragraph:

    (a) Comply fully in spirit and in practice with the provisions of the Universal Declaration of Human Rights;

    (b) Release all Namibian political prisoners, including all those imprisoned or detained in connection with offences under so-called internal security laws, whether such Namibians have been charged or tried or are held without charge and whether held in Namibia or South Africa;

    (c) Abolish the application in Namibia of all racially discriminatory and politically repressive laws and practices, particularly bantustans and homelands;

    (d) Accord unconditionally to all Namibians currently in exile for political reasons full facilities for return to their country without risk of arrest, detention, intimidation or imprisonment;

12. *Decides* to remain seized of the matter and to meet on or before 31 August 1976 for the purpose of reviewing South Africa's compliance with the terms of this resolution and, in the event of non-compliance by South Africa, for the purpose of considering the appropriate measures to be taken under the Charter.

Namibia: S/15287

United Nations

Letter (S/15287) dated 12 July 1982 from the Representatives of Canada, France, the Federal Republic of Germany, the United Kingdom of Great Britain and Northern Ireland and the United States of America to the Secretary-General

On instructions from our Governments we have the honour to transmit to you the text of Principles concerning the Constituent Assembly and the Constitution for an independent Namibia put forward by our Governments to the parties concerned in the negotiations for the implementation of the proposal for a settlement of the Namibian situation (S/12636) in accordance with Security Council resolution 435(1978).

We have pleasure in informing you that all parties to the negotiation now accept these Principles. Our Governments believe that a decision on the method to be employed to elect the Constituent Assembly should be made in accordance with the provision of Council resolution 435(1978). All parties are agreed that this issue must be settled in accordance with the terms of resolution 435(1978) and that the issue must not cause delay in the implementation of that resolution. In this regard, our Governments are in consultation with all parties...

Annex

Principles concerning the Constituent Assembly and the Constitution for an Independent Namibia

A. Constituent Assembly

1. In accordance with United Nations Security Council resolution 435(1978), elections will be held to select a Constituent Assembly which will adopt a Constitution for an independent Namibia. The Constitution will determine the organization and powers of all levels of government.

■ Every adult Namibian will be eligible, without discrimination or fear of intimidation from any source, to vote, campaign and stand for election to the Constituent Assembly.

■ Voting will be by secret ballot, with provisions made for those who cannot read or write.

■ The date for the beginning of the electoral campaign, the date of elections, the electoral system, the preparation of voters rolls and other aspects of electoral procedures will be promptly decided upon so as to give all political parties and interested persons, without regard to their political views, a full and fair opportunity to organize and participate in the electoral process.

■ Full freedom of speech, assembly, movement and press shall be guaranteed.

■ The electoral system will seek to ensure fair representation in the Constituent Assembly to different political parties which gain substantial support in the elections.

2. The Constituent Assembly will formulate the Constitution for an independent Namibia in accordance with the principles in part B below and will adopt the Constitution as a whole by a two-thirds majority of its total membership.

B. Principles for a Constitution for an Independent Namibia

1. Namibia will be a unitary, sovereign and democratic State.

2. The Constitution will be the supreme law of the State. It may be amended only by a designated process involving the legislature or votes cast in a popular referendum, or both.

3. The Constitution will determine the organization and powers of all levels of government. It will provide for a system of government with three branches: an elected executive branch which will be responsible to the legislative branch; a legislative branch to be elected by universal and equal suffrage which will be responsible for the passage of all laws; and an independent judicial branch which will be responsible for the interpretation

Appendix VIII

of the Constitution and for ensuring its supremacy and the authority of the law. The executive and legislative branches will be constituted by periodic and genuine elections which will be held by secret vote.

4. The electoral system will be consistent with the principles in A.1 above.

5. There will be a declaration of fundamental rights, which will include the rights to life, personal liberty and freedom of movement; to freedom of conscience; to freedom of expression, including freedom of speech and a free press; to freedom of assembly and association, including political parties and trade unions; to due process and equality before the law; to protection from arbitrary deprivation of private property or deprivation of private property without just compensation; and to freedom from racial, ethnic, religious or sexual discrimination.

The declaration of rights will be consistent with the provisions of the Universal Declaration of Human Rights. Aggrieved individuals will be entitled to have the courts adjudicate and enforce these rights.

6. It will be forbidden to create criminal offences with retrospective effect or to provide for increased penalties with retrospective effect.

7. Provision will be made for the balanced structuring of the public service, the police service and the defence services and for equal access by all to recruitment of these services. The fair administration of personnel policy in relation to these services will be assured by appropriate independent bodies.

8. Provision will be made for the establishment of elected councils for local or regional administration, or both.

Appendix IX 115

ANNEX

NAMIBIA: INFORMAL CHECK LIST

1. The elections will be under the supervision and control of the United Nations (UN) and the UN Special Representative (UNSR) must be satisfied at each stage of that process as to the fairness and appropriateness of all measures affecting the political process at all levels of administration before such measures take effect.
2. Full freedom of speech, assembly, movement and press shall be guaranteed.
3. All legislation—including proclamations by the Administrator-General (AG)—that are inconsistent with the plan must be repealed. All discriminatory or restrictive laws, regulations or administrative measures which might abridge or inhibit free and fair elections must be repealed.
4. The AG must make arrangements for the release, prior to the beginning of the electoral campaign, of all Namibian political prisoners or political detainees held by the South African authorities.
5. All Namibians in exile shall have the right of peaceful return so that they can participate fully and freely in the elections without risk of arrest, detention, intimidation or imprisonment.
6. The UN has made provisions to finance the return of these detainees and those in exile ($33 million in original UN budget estimate).
7. Council of Ministers and National Assembly: UN Security Council resolution (SCR) 439 declares that all unilateral measures taken by the illegal administration in Namibia in relation to the transfer of power are null and void. The December 1978 elections held in Namibia are null and void. No recognition has been accorded either by the UN or any Member State (other than South Africa) to any representatives or organs established by that process. Accordingly only the Administrator-General and UNSR will exercise authority during the transition period within Namibia consistent with the settlement plan and will do so impartially.
8. Impartiality provisions to be covered by final Security Council enabling resolution: the resolution should emphasize responsibility of all concerned to co-operate to ensure impartial implementation of the settlement plan. The Secretary-General and UN bodies should be directed to act impartially according to the settlement plan and the Secretary-General should be directed to:
    (a) initiate a review of all programmes administered by organs of the UN with respect to Namibia to ensure that they are administered on an impartial basis;
    (b) seek the co-operation of the executive heads of the specialized agencies and other organisations and bodies within the UN system to ensure that their activities with respect to Namibia are conducted impartially.
9. At the Security Council meeting to authorize implementation of SCR 435, speakers should be kept to a minimum. Specifically, none of the parties to the election or to the cease-fire would speak.
10. Consideration of the question of Namibia at the regular General Assembly should be suspended during the transition period.
11. The UN will not provide funds for SWAPO or any other party during the transition period.
12. The UN Council for Namibia should refrain from engaging in all public activities once the Security Council meets to authorize implementation.
13. The Commissioner for Namibia and his Office should suspend all political activities during the transition period.
14. SWAPO will voluntarily forego the exercise of the special privileges granted to it by the General Assembly, including participation as an official observer in the General Assembly and in other bodies and conferences within the UN system.
15. Monitoring the South West Africa Police Force: the UN Plan provides that the primary responsibility for maintaining law and order in Namibia during the transition period shall rest with the existing police forces. The AG, to the satisfaction of the UNSR, shall ensure the good conduct of the police forces and shall take the necessary action to ensure their suitability for continued employment during the transition period. The UNSR shall make arrangements when appropriate for UN personnel to accompany the police forces in the

discharge of their duties. The police forces would be limited to the carrying of small arms in the normal performance of their duties. The UN Plan also provides that the UNSR will take steps to guarantee against the possibility of intimidation or interference with the electoral process from whatever quarter. The Secretary-General has provided that designated personnel will be at the disposal of the UNSR to ensure that these monitoring responsibilities will be satisfactorily performed. For reasons of safety and affectiveness, these tasks will be performed by civilian personnel who are professionally qualified. The number of UN personnel to monitor the police appropriate to the tasks they are expected to perform will be kept under continuous review.

16. South West Africa Territorial Force (SWATF): The UN Plan specifies that the United Nations Transition Assistance Group (UNTAG) military component will monitor "the demobilization of citizen forces, commandos, and ethnic forces, and the dismantling of their command structure". UNTAG will monitor the demobilization of SWATF and the dismantling of its command structure.

17. Composition of the UNTAG military component will be decided by the Security Council on the recommendation of the Secretary-General after due consultations. Final arrangements for the military component of UNTAG including monitoring of SWAPO facilities in Angola and Zambia will be decided by the Secretary-General, after due consultation.

PRINCIPLES FOR A PEACEFUL SETTLEMENT IN SOUTHWESTERN AFRICA

(Approved by the South African Government on 18 July 1988)

The Government of the People's Republic of Angola, the Republic of Cuba, and the Republic of South Africa have reached agreement on a set of essential principles to establish the basis for peace in the southwestern region of Africa. They recognize that each of these principles is indispensable to a comprehensive settlement.

A. Implementation of resolution 435/78 of the Security Council of the United Nations. The parties shall agree upon and recommend to the Secretary-General of the United Nations a date for the commencement of implementation of UNSCR 435/78.

B. The Governments of the People's Republic of Angola and of the Republic of South Africa shall, in conformity with the dispositions of resolution 435/78 of the Security Council of the United Nations, co-operate with the Secretary-General with a view towards ensuring the independence of Namibia through free and fair elections, abstaining from any action that could prevent the execution of said resolution.

C. Redeployment toward the North and the staged and total withdrawal of Cuban troops from the territory of the People's Republic of Angola on the basis of an agreement between the People's Republic of Angola and the Republic of Cuba and the decision of both states to solicit the on-site verification of that withdrawal by the Security Council of the United Nations.

D. Respect for the sovereignty, sovereign equality, and independence of states and for territorial integrity and inviolability of borders.

E. Non-interference in the internal affairs of states.

F. Abstention from the threat and utilization of force against the territorial integrity and independence of states.

G. The acceptance of the responsibility of states not to allow their territory to be used for acts of war, aggression, or violence against other states.

H. Reaffirmation of the right of the peoples of the southwestern region of Africa to self-determination, independence, and equality of rights.

I. Verification and monitoring of compliance with the obligations resulting from the agreements that may be established.

J. Commitment to comply in good faith with the obligations undertaken in the agreements that may be established and to resolve the differences via negotiations.

K. Recognition of the role of the Permanent Members of the Security Council of the United Nations as guarantors for the implementation of agreements that may be established.

L. The right of each state to peace, development, and social progress.

M. African and international co-operation for the settlement of the problems of the development of the southwestern region of Africa.

N. Recognition of the mediating role of the Government of the United States of America.

Appendix XI

**UNITED
NATIONS**

S

Security Council

Distr.
GENERAL

S/20566
4 April 1989

ORIGINAL: ENGLISH

LETTER DATED 4 APRIL 1989 FROM THE PERMANENT REPRESENTATIVE OF SOUTH
AFRICA TO THE UNITED NATIONS ADDRESSED TO THE SECRETARY-GENERAL

I have the honour to refer to the undertakings which SWAPO made to you
concerning its participation in the cessation of hostilities in terms of the
Protocol of Geneva, signed on 8 August 1988 by representatives of the People's
Republic of Angola, the Republic of Cuba and the Republic of South Africa as well
as the cease-fire provided for in Security Council resolution 632 (1989).

In the light of SWAPO's incursion into Namibian territory on 31 March 1989 and
subsequent escalation of the resulting conflict situation in defiance of Security
Council resolutions 435 (1978), 629 (1989) and 632 (1989), I have been instructed
to provide you with the attached copy of the Protocol, with the request that it be
circulated as a document of the Security Council.

(Signed) Jeremy B. SHEARAR
Permanent Representative

/...

S/20566
English
Page 2

Annex

Protocol of Geneva

Delegations representing the Governments of the People's Republic of Angola/
Republic of Cuba, and the Republic of South Africa, meeting in Geneva, Switzerland,
2-5 August 1988, with the mediation of Dr. Chester A. Crocker, Assistant Secretary
of State for African Affairs, United States of America, have agreed as follows:

1.   Each side agrees to recommend to the Secretary-General of the United Nations
that 1 November 1988 be established as the date for implementation of UNSCR 435/78.

2.   Each side agrees to the establishment of a target date for signature of the
tripartite agreement among Angola, South Africa, and Cuba not later than
10 September 1988.

3.   Each side agrees that a schedule acceptable to all parties for the
redeployment toward the North and the staged and total withdrawal of Cuban troops
from Angola must be established by Angola and Cuba, who will request on-site
verification by the Security Council of the United Nations. The parties accept
1 September 1988 as the target date for reaching agreement on that schedule and all
related matters.

4.   The complete withdrawal of South African forces from Angola shall begin not
later than 10 August 1988 and be completed not later than 1 September 1988.

5.   The parties undertake to adopt the necessary measures of restraint in order to
maintain the existing de facto cessation of hostilities. South Africa stated its
willingness to convey this commitment in writing to the Secretary-General of the
United Nations. Angola and Cuba shall urge SWAPO to proceed likewise as a step
prior to the ceasefire contemplated in resolution 435/78 which will be established
prior to 1 November 1988. Angola and Cuba shall use their good offices so that,
once the total withdrawal of South African troops from Angola is completed, and
within the context also of the cessation of hostilities in Namibia, SWAPO's forces
will be deployed to the north of the 16th parallel. The parties deemed it
appropriate that, during the period before 1 November 1988, a representative of the
United Nations Secretary-General be present in Luanda to take cognizance of any
disputes relative to the cessation of hostilities and agreed that the combined
military committee contemplated in paragraph 9 can be an appropriate venue for
reviewing complaints of this nature that may arise.

6.   As of 10 August 1988, no Cuban troops will deploy or be south of the line
Chitado-Ruacana-Calueque-Naulila-Cuamato-N'Giva. Cuba furthermore stated that upon
completion of the withdrawal of the South African troops from Angola not later than
1 September 1988 and the restoration by the People's Republic of Angola of its
sovereignty over its international boundaries, the Cuban troops will not take part
in offensive operations in the territory that lies east of meridian 17 and south of
parallel 15 degrees, 30 minutes, provided that they are not subject to harassment.

/...

Appendix XI

S/20566
English
Page 3

7. Following the complete withdrawal of South African forces from Angola, the Government of Angola shall guarantee measures for the provision of water and power supply to Namibia.

8. With a view toward minimizing the risk of battlefield incidents and facilitating exchange of technical information related to implementation of the agreements reached, direct communications shall be established not later than 20 August 1988 between the respective military commanders at appropriate headquarters along the Angola/Namibia border.

9. Each side recognizes that the period from 1 September 1988, by which time South African forces will have completed their withdrawal from Angola, and the date established for implementation of UNSCR 435, is a period of particular sensitivity, for which specific guidelines for military activities are presently lacking. In the interest of maintaining the ceasefire and maximizing the conditions for the orderly introduction of UNTAG, the sides agree to establish a combined military committee to develop additional practical measures to build confidence and reduce the risk of unintended incidents. They invite United States membership on the committee.

10. Each side will act in accordance with the Governors Island principles, including paragraph E (non-interference in the internal affairs of states) and paragraph G (the acceptance of the responsibility of states not to allow their territory to be used for acts of war, aggression, or violence against other states).

FOR THE GOVERNMENT OF THE PEOPLE'S REPUBLIC OF ANGOLA:

FOR THE GOVERNMENT OF THE REPUBLIC OF CUBA:

FOR THE GOVERNMENT OF THE REPUBLIC OF SOUTH AFRICA:

Geneva, 5 August 1988

**UNITED
NATIONS**

S

Security Council

Distr.
GENERAL

S/20129
17 August 1988

ORIGINAL: ENGLISH

LETTER DATED 17 AUGUST 1988 FROM THE REPRESENTATIVES OF TUNISIA
AND ZAMBIA ADDRESSED TO THE SECRETARY-GENERAL

We, the representatives of the States mentioned below, have the honour to transmit the enclosed letter dated 12 August 1988 addressed to Your Excellency by Dr. Sam Nujoma, the President of the South West Africa People's Organization (SWAPO).

We request that the enclosure be circulated as a document of the Security Council.

(Signed) I. Z. CHABALA
Charge d'affaires a.i.
Permanent Mission of the Republic
of Zambia to the United Nations

(Signed) M. Ahmed GHEZAL
Ambassador/Permanent Representative
Permanent Mission of Tunisia to
the United Nations

Appendix XII

<u>Annex</u>

<u>Letter dated 12 August 1988 from the President of the South West
Africa People's Organization addressed to the Secretary-General</u>

It is now nearly 10 years since the United Nations Security Council resolution
435 (1978) was adopted.

In my letter dated 8 September 1978 addressed to your predecessor, I stated
SWAPO's views on the various aspects of the Secretary-General's report, containing
the United Nations Plan, submitted to the Security Council pursuant to the relevant
provisions of resolution 435 (1978) concerning the decolonization of Namibia.

During the ensuing years since the adoption of resolution 435 (1978), I have
on many occasions and in various places reiterated SWAPO's unassailable position of
goodwill, flexibility and a spirit of compromise whenever serious efforts were made
aimed at ensuring progress and speeding up the independence of Namibia, through the
implementation of the said resolution.

It is hardly my intention here to overstate the case about SWAPO's credibility
which is well-known to all men of reason and honesty. But I can say in full
confidence that it has all along been SWAPO's willingness to make the necessary
concessions, while at the same time remaining committed to the letter and spirit of
Security Council resolutions 385 (1976) and 435 (1978), that the continuing efforts
to implement these seminal resolutions are still on course, in spite of many years
of despicable provocations, repeated demonstrations of bad faith, a lack of
sincerity and endless recourse to condemnable prevarication on the part of South
Africa.

Since Your Excellency's assumption, in 1982, of the High Office of the
Secretary-General of the United Nations, I have continued to send numerous
communications to you in which I have time and again reiterated SWAPO's readiness
to co-operate with the United Nations and in particular with you and your staff
concerning the signing of a cease-fire agreement with South Africa as the first
vital step in the implementation of the United Nations Plan for the independence of
Namibia, as endorsed in resolution 435 (1978).

In this connection, I would like to recall Your Excellency's latest reports to
the Security Council contained in documents (S/18767) of 31 March 1987 and
(S/19234) of 27 October 1987. These reports, as the previous ones had done,
clearly and categorically corroborated my contention that SWAPO has never been
found equivocating on any serious matter relating to cease-fire, composition and
emplacement of UNTAG in Namibia or willingness to co-operate with the United
Nations.

In paragraph 5 of resolution 601 (1987), the Council decided "to authorize the
United Nations Secretary-General to proceed to arrange a cease-fire between South
Africa and the South West Africa People's Organization in order to undertake
administrative and other practical steps necessary for the emplacement of the
United Nations Transition Assistance Group (UNTAG)".

/...

S/20129
English
Page 3

Once again, immediately following the adoption of that resolution, I promptly sent a letter dated 1 November 1987 to Your Excellency reassuring you of SWAPO's readiness to sign and observe a cease-fire, on the basis of resolution 435, provided that the South African régime is going to have to do likewise.

Now we have reached a most decisive stage concerning the independence of Namibia which demands of us all to make earnest efforts, in good faith, towards hastening the peace process in the South West African region.

Your Excellency, it is with this deep concern in mind that I have decided to write to you at this time.

SWAPO, which derives its legitimacy from the persistent and overwhelming support of the oppressed people of Namibia as the leader in the liberation struggle, has earned the universal recognition as the sole and authentic representative of the fighting masses of our embattled country.

It is this popular and continuing support from the masses which assures the rank and file of our movement that the thousands of our best sons and daughters who have sacrificed and are sacrificing their precious lives in the struggle shall not have died in vain.

The legacy of their courage and heroism is what gives us confidence and strengthens our determination to continue providing leadership with courage and imagination to act decisively in war and in peace with the sole purposes of saving lives, defending the interest of our people and seizing all favourable opportunities to give back to them the power to exercise their inalienable right to self-determination, freedom and independence.

Against this background of both setbacks and of tremendous progress in the heroic struggle, I wish to inform Your Excellency that SWAPO has by its own sovereign and unilateral decision, as a national liberation movement, in accordance with the spirit of the Geneva agreement reached by the Parties participating in the Quatripartite talks, committed itself to take the necessary steps to help make the peace process in the South West African Region irreversible and successful.

In this context, SWAPO has agreed to comply with the commencement of the cessation of all hostile acts which started as of 10 August 1988 in Angola. By the same token, SWAPO will be ready to continue to abide by this agreement until the formal cease-fire, under resolution 435, is signed between SWAPO and South Africa, thereby triggering the implementation process.

The cessation of SWAPO's combat actions against the South African Forces in Namibia will only hold provided South Africa also shows the necessary political will to do the same.

In order to enhance the prospects for peace and tranquillity in the country and to create appropriate conditions for the speedy implementation of resolution 435, South Africa should be called upon to refrain from committing any acts of repression against SWAPO members and supporters inside Namibia during this period.

Appendix XII

S/20129
English
Page 4

In welcoming the fixing of 1 November 1988 as the firm date for the commencement of the implementation of resolution 435, SWAPO would like to urge Your Excellency to avail your good offices of the opportunity created in the current preliminary phase of the cessation of acts of hostilities by initiating consultations with the parties concerned.

(Signed)   Sam NUJOMA
President of SWAPO

PROTOCOL OF BRAZZAVILLE

Delegations representing the Governments of the People's Republic of Angola, the Republic of Cuba, and the Republic of South Africa,

Meeting in Brazzaville with the mediation of the Government of the United States of America,

Expressing their deep appreciation to the President of the People's Republic of the Congo, Colonel Denis Sassou-Nguesso, for his indispensable contribution to the cause of peace in southwestern Africa and for the hospitality extended to the delegations by the Government of the People's Republic of the Congo,

Confirming their commitment to act in accordance with the Principles for a peaceful settlement in southwestern Africa, initialled at New York on 13 July 1988 and approved by their respective Governments on 20 July 1988, each of which is indispensable to a comprehensive settlement; with the understandings reached at Geneva on 5 August 1988 that are not superseded by this document; and with the agreement reached at Geneva on 15 November 1988 for the redeployment to the North and the staged and total withdrawal of Cuban troops from Angola,

Urging the international community to provide economic and financial support for the implementation of all aspects of this settlement,

Agree as follows:

1. The parties agree to recommend to the Secretary-General of the United Nations that 1 April 1989 be established as the date for implementation of UNSCR 435/78.
2. The parties agree to meet on 22 December 1988 in New York for signature of the tripartite agreement and for signature by Angola and Cuba of their bilateral agreement. By the date of signature, Angola and Cuba shall have reached agreement with the Secretary-General of the United Nations on verification arrangements to be approved by the Security Council.
3. The parties agree to exchange the prisoners of war upon signature of the tripartite agreement.
4. The parties agree to establish a Joint Commission in accordance with the annex attached to this protocol.

FOR THE GOVERNMENT OF THE PEOPLE'S REPUBLIC OF ANGOLA:

FOR THE GOVERNMENT OF THE REPUBLIC OF CUBA:

FOR THE GOVERNMENT OF THE REPUBLIC OF SOUTH AFRICA.

Brazzaville, 13 December 1988

Appendix XIV

ANNEXURES

[1]

AGREEMENT AMONG
THE PEOPLE'S REPUBLIC OF ANGOLA,
THE REPUBLIC OF CUBA,
AND
THE REPUBLIC OF SOUTH AFRICA

The governments of the People's Republic of Angola, the Republic of Cuba, and the Republic of South Africa, hereinafter designated as "the Parties",

Taking into account the "Principles for a peaceful settlement in southwestern Africa", approved by the Parties on 20 July 1988, and the subsequent negotiations with respect to the implementation of these Principles, each of which is indispensable to a comprehensive settlement,

Considering the acceptance by the Parties of the implementation of United Nations Security Council resolution 435 (1978), adopted on 29 September 1978, hereinafter designated as "UNSCR 435/78",

Considering the conclusion of the bilateral agreement between the People's Republic of Angola and the Republic of Cuba providing for the redeployment toward the North and the staged and total withdrawal of Cuban troops from the territory of the People's Republic of Angola,

Recognizing the role of the United Nations Security Council in implementing UNSCR 435/78 and in supporting the implementation of the present agreement,

Affirming the sovereignty, sovereign equality, and independence of all states of southwestern Africa,

Affirming the principle of non-interference in the internal affairs of states,

Affirming the principle of abstention from the threat or use of force against the territorial integrity or political independence of states,

Reaffirming the right of the peoples of the southwestern region of Africa to self-determination, independence, and equality of rights, and of the states of southwestern Africa to peace, development, and social progress,

Urging African and international co-operation for the settlement of the problems of the development of the southwestern region of Africa,

Expressing their appreciation for the mediating role of the Government of the United States of America,

Desiring to contribute to the establishment of peace and security in southwestern Africa,

Agree to the provisions set forth below.

(1) The Parties shall immediately request the Secretary-General of the United Nations to seek authority from the Security Council to commence implementation of UNSCR 435/78 on 1 April 1989.

(2) All military forces of the Republic of South Africa shall depart Namibia in accordance with UNSCR 435/78.

(3) Consistent with the provisions of UNSCR 435/78, the Republic of South Africa and the People's Republic of Angola shall co-operate with the Secretary-General to ensure the independence of Namibia through free and fair elections and shall abstain from any action that could prevent the execution of UNSCR 435/78. The Parties shall respect the territorial integrity and inviolability of borders of Namibia and shall ensure that their territories are not used by any state, organization, or person in connection with acts of war, aggression, or violence against the territorial integrity or inviolability of borders of Namibia or any other action which could prevent the execution of UNSCR 435/78.

(4) The People's Republic of Angola and the Republic of Cuba shall implement the bilateral agreement, signed on the date of signature of this agreement, providing for the redeployment toward the North and the staged and total withdrawal of Cuban troops from

the territory of the People's Republic of Angola, and the arrangements made with the Security Council of the United Nations for the on-site verification of that withdrawal.

(5) Consistent with their obligations under the Charter of the United Nations, the Parties shall refrain from the threat or use of force, and shall ensure that their respective territories are not used by any state, organization, or person in connection with any acts of war, aggression, or violence, against the territorial integrity, inviolability of borders, or independence of any state of southwestern Africa.

(6) The Parties shall respect the principle of non-interference in the internal affairs of the states of southwestern Africa.

(7) The Parties shall comply in good faith with all obligations undertaken in this agreement and shall resolve through negotiation and in a spirit of co-operation any disputes with respect to the interpretation or implementation thereof.

(8) This agreement shall enter into force upon signature.

Signed at New York in triplicate in the Portuguese, Spanish and English languages, each language being equally authentic, this 22nd day of December 1988.

FOR THE PEOPLE'S
REPUBLIC OF ANGOLA:

FOR THE REPUBLIC OF
CUBA:

FOR THE REPUBLIC OF
SOUTH AFRICA:

CODE OF CONDUCT
FOR POLITICAL PARTIES DURING PRESENT ELECTION CAMPAIGN

On Tuesday 12 September 1989 nine Namibian political parties signed an agreement among themselves. It establishes a Code of Conduct which they have pledged to respect during the coming electoral campaign. They have also agreed to issue directives to their members and supporters to observe this Code, and to take other necessary steps to ensure that its terms are respected. They, and I, have also agreed to publicise this Code throughout Namibia by all the various means at our disposal.

I have been deeply impressed by the attitudes of restraint, constructiveness and flexibility shown by the parties in concluding this agreement. It is an important and historic achievement on the long road that has led to the prospect, soon to be realised, of free and fair elections for an independent Namibia. It is also a significant step towards national reconciliation.

Martti Ahtisaari, Special Representative of the Secretary-General

An essential part of free and fair elections is freedom of political campaigning. Everyone has the right to put forward their political principles and ideas, without threat or fear, to every other person, without exception. But freedom of political campaigning also carries responsibilities, including the duty to accept every other person's freedom to campaign.

The Namibian political parties whose names are subscribed to this document, meeting together in Windhoek under the chairmanship of the Special Representative of the Secretary-General of the United Nations on 12 September 1989, have agreed as follows:

▶ 1. Intimidation, in any form, is unacceptable and will be expressly forbidden by the parties in directives to their members and supporters.

▶ 2. Party leaders will instruct their members and supporters that no weapon of any kind, including any traditional weapon, may be brought to any political rally, meeting, march or other demonstration.

▶ 3. Parties will notify UNTAG-CIVPOL as well as SWAPOL in advance of their planned meetings and other rallies.

▶ 4. All practical steps will be taken by parties to avoid holding rallies, meetings, marches or demonstrations close to one another at the same time. Party leaders undertake to co-operate in applying this principle in good faith and in a reasonable spirit should any coincidence of time or venue arise.

▶ 5. Speakers at political rallies will at all times avoid using language which threatens or incites violence in any form against any other person or group of persons. Parties will not issue pamphlets, newsletters or posters, whether officially or anonymously, which contain inflammatory language or material.

▶ 6. All parties will consistently emphasize, both to their supporters and also to voters in general, that there will be a secret ballot, and that consequently no one will know how any individual may have voted.

▶ 7. Party members and supporters will not disrupt other parties' rallies, meetings, marches or demonstrations.

▶ 8. Party members and supporters will not seek to obstruct other persons from attending the political rallies of other parties.

▶ 9. Party members and supporters will not plagiarize symbols of other parties, or steal, disfigure or destroy political or campaign materials of other parties.

▶ 10. Party leaders will use their good offices to seek to ensure reasonable freedom of access by all political parties to all potential voters, whether they be at farms, on state-owned properties, in villages, or at secondary reception centres. They will also seek to ensure that such potential voters wishing to participate in related political activities have freedom to do so. This may, where necessary, take place outside working hours.

▶ 11. Parties will establish effective lines of communication to one another at headquarters, regional and district levels, and will appoint liaison personnel who will be constantly on call to deal with any problems that may arise.

▶ 12. Parties will meet on a fortnightly basis under the chairmanship of UNTAG regional directors or centre heads to discuss all matters of concern relating to the election campaign. A standing committee of party leaders at headquarters will meet on a fortnightly basis under the chairmanship of the Special Representative or his Deputy to deal with such matters on a nation-wide basis. An observer from the Office of the AG will be invited to attend the meeting of the standing committee. Emergency meetings will be convened as and when necessary.

▶ 13. All allegations of intimidation and other unlawful conduct in the election campaign will be brought to the attention of the nearest UNTAG-CIVPOL and SWAPOL stations or patrols.

▶ 14. Party leaders will issue directives to their members and supporters to observe this Code of Conduct, and take all other necessary steps to ensure compliance.

▶ 15. It is stated in the Settlement Proposal that: "The elections will be under the supervision and control of the United Nations in that, as a condition to the conduct of the electoral process, the elections themselves and the certification of their results, the United Nations Special Representative will have to satisfy himself at each stage as to the fairness and appropriateness of all measures affecting the political process at all levels of administration before such measures take effect." Party leaders undertake to honour the outcome of free and fair elections so certified by the Special Representative of the Secretary-General of the United Nations.

▶ 16. The Special Representative and party leaders undertake to publicise this Code of Conduct throughout Namibia by all means at their disposal.

The Namibian political parties whose names are subscribed below accept and endorse this Code of Conduct as binding upon them. They agree that alleged violations will be brought to and considered by the Standing Committee referred to in paragraph 12 above.

NAME OF PARTY	NAME OF REPRESENTATIVE	SIGNATURE
Action Christian National	J.M. de Wet	
Democratic Turnhalle Alliance	F.J. Kozonguizi	
Federal Convention of Namibia	H. Diergaardt	
Namibia Christian Democratic Party	W. Adam	
Namibia National Front	I. Uirab	
National Patriotic Front of Namibia	E. van Zijl	
South West Africa People's Organization	H.G. Geingob	
SWAPO-Democrats	for A. Shipanga	
United Democratic Front	Justus Garoeb	

In the presence of the Special Representative of the Secretary-General,

Martti Ahtisaari

UNTAG Headquarters,
Windhoek, 12 September 1989

 UNTAG

AKSIE CHRISTELIK NASIONAAL	ACN		
CHRISTIAN DEMOCRATIC ACTION FOR SOCIAL JUSTICE	CDA		
D.T.A. VAN NAMIBIË	DTA		
FEDERAL CONVENTION OF NAMIBIA	FCN		
NAMIBIA NATIONAL DEMOCRATIC PARTY	NNDP		
NAMIBIA NATIONAL FRONT	NNF		
NATIONAL PATRIOTIC FRONT OF NAMIBIA	NPF		
SWAPO-DEMOCRATS	SWAPO-D		
SWAPO OF NAMIBIA	SWAPO		
UNITED DEMOCRATIC FRONT OF NAMIBIA	UDF		

Appendix XVII

Namibian Election: Summary Results by Electoral District

Electoral district number	Name of district	ACN	CDA	DTA	FCN	NNDP	NNF	NPF	SWAPO-D	SWAPO	UDF	Reject	Total votes cast	Total valid votes
01	Bethanie	301	32	1,314	55	4	8	15	16	461	87	44	2,337	2,293
02	Damaraland	175	28	2,579	34	9	109	62	25	4,204	7,838	152	15,215	15,063
03	Gobabis	1,940	158	11,684	173	50	391	377	59	2,458	442	379	18,111	17,732
04	Grootfontein	1,606	115	8,818	236	32	66	376	51	6,417	1,319	566	19,602	19,036
05	Hereroland	68	89	9,880	193	33	705	1,935	40	2,353	100	209	15,605	15,396
06	Kaokoland	64	91	8,180	120	70	48	2,480	24	1,330	71	316	12,794	12,478
07	Karasburg	4,820	54	10,068	367	30	40	152	39	2,378	739	126	18,813	18,687
08	Karibib	406	24	1,989	67	2	56	161	14	2,244	1,533	86	6,582	6,496
09	Kavango	527	449	24,817	401	179	151	497	319	30,755	1,336	1,995	61,426	59,431
10	Keetmanshoop	1,458	100	9,249	335	58	432	209	113	5,496	1,518	301	19,269	18,968
11	Lüderitz	521	17	2,138	89	14	218	67	26	7,753	390	45	11,278	11,233
12	Maltahöhe	388	15	668	161	13	8	14	9	848	383	71	2,578	2,507
13	Mariental	1,467	85	7,665	403	26	77	101	29	3,024	1,036	169	14,082	13,913
14	Okahandja	672	42	4,273	56	9	81	334	23	3,718	1,142	30	10,380	10,350
15	Omaruru	213	40	2,959	48	5	206	318	24	1,281	589	89	5,772	5,683
16	Oos-Caprivi	104	168	13,786	436	44	44	687	93	10,415	556	673	27,006	26,333
17	Otjiwarongo	699	49	5,213	81	12	134	114	19	4,020	1,835	142	12,318	12,176
18	Outjo	765	37	3,072	88	3	31	52	13	1,197	1,483	163	6,904	6,741
19	Ovambo	465	489	10,745	150	214	95	505	1,706	225,621	5,167	3,014	248,171	245,157
20	Rehoboth	127	66	7,746	5,010	84	304	243	48	3,015	462	251	17,356	17,105
21	Swakopmund	1,271	32	5,931	395	5	241	145	64	14,123	1,736	140	24,083	23,943
22	Tsumeb	922	36	4,028	96	11	46	72	57	7,254	1,202	148	13,872	13,724
23	Windhoek	4,749	279	34,730	1,458	77	1,853	1,777	350	44,202	6,910	749	97,134	96,385
	Grand totals:	23,728	2,495	191,532	10,452	984	5,344	10,693	3,161	384,567	37,874	9,858	680,688	670,830